Home Based Travel Affiliate

Turn Your Website into a Virtual Money Machine

By Tom Ogg

HomeBasedTravelAffiliate.com

Published by
Tom Ogg & Associates
P.O. Box 2398
Valley Center, California 82082
1-760-751-1007
Fax 1-760-751-1309
TomOgg@aol.com
http://www.HomeBasedTravelAffiliate.com

Printed June, 2007, San Diego, California

Printed in the United States of America

ISBN# 1-888290-11-0
10 9 8 7 6 5 4 3 2 1

Because laws and interpretations change, and Because a written sentence, or paragraph may be Subject to different interpretations, this book Is sold with the specific understanding that the author Is neither a member of the bar in any state, nor a licensed CPA and is not offering or rendering legal or accounting Advice. Any reference made to those topics within the book should be addressed to members of those professions hired as such.

The author does not assume, and hereby disclaims any liability to any party for all loss and damage caused by Errors and omissions in *"Home-Based Travel Affiliate"* whether such errors and omissions result from negligence, accident or any other cause. While every effort has been made to complete the most current information available at press time, the author urges readers to consult specialists for up-to-the-minute information regarding any topic in this book.

Foreword

I took numerous cruises during the years and started a hobby website so that I could write reviews for others to read if they were interested. I found that people also wanted to submit reviews of their own, so the site started growing. I really didn't care too much about it, but because I cruised by myself most of the time, I enjoyed writing the reviews of the ships and ports. It gave me a purpose beyond that of just being a seminar facilitator. My son was in College and needed an income, so I gave him the job of editing and publishing the reviews when readers submitted them. What started out as an insignificant amount of pay for doing so turned into a meaningful monthly amount. So I decided to see if there was a way to get the site to generate some income without having to invest much time into it.

I visited a Webmaster's forum that occasionally frequented and posted the question "Does anyone have any ideas how to generate an income from a site that has about 8,000 pageviews a day?" I immediately received a response, "Have you thought about AdSense?" After clearing up what AdSense was and where to get it, I went to Google's site and signed up. That was on October 2nd, 2003. When I logged onto my account the next morning, I hoped to see that I had made a couple of dollars. I had made $63.01 and couldn't believe it. The next day (October 3rd, 2003) I made $105.07 and then 3 days later on what turned out to be the best day of the week for me, I made $166.68.

I couldn't believe my eyes! I made a total of $3,992.96 in October of 2003 and it wasn't even a full month. So for fun, I started to fiddle with AdSense and the site itself. I tried all kinds of things to increase my click-through rate, pageviews and so on. Over the next couple of years I was able to build the site from the 8,000 daily pageviews it was receiving in October of 2003 into approximately 65,000 daily pageviews. I also grew the affiliate revenue that the sites generated into a six-figure income.

Sometime in January of 2006 I received a telephone call from someone that wanted to buy the sites. While I had received a good number of inquiries, they were always bottom feeders looking for a bargain. I gave them basic information about the site and told them to make me an offer if they were interested and they did. I sold the sites on February 1st, 2006 for what most people think is a ton of cash based simply on its affiliate productivity.

This book is about what I learned during the journey while building the sites and affiliate revenue. Today, I am a firm believer in the opportunities that Web 2.0 offers us all.

Travel is a wonderful segment of global commerce and one that will not only reward you financially, but will allow you to discover new experiences that add to the very essence of your personality. I hope you make millions of dollars with this information and get to travel the globe as I have done. I wish you the best of luck.

Tom Ogg

Table of Contents

Chapter Seven
The Power of Community

Chapter Eight
Google's AdSense, Start Your Money Machine

Chapter Nine
Travel Affiliate Programs

Chapter Ten
Marketing Your Website

Chapter Eleven

SEO, Search Engine Optimization

Chapter Twelve

Bringing it All Together

Glossary of Terms

Chapter One

Understanding Global Commerce

My, how the world has changed! When I was a teenager, we would go surfing without knowing the surf conditions taking the chance that there would be waves. When we hit it just right, we had the waves all to ourselves, until the word spread that there was a new swell. Today, I can track storm and ocean activity the world over and show up at my favorite break right on time to get the best part of the event at the perfect tide. I can track storms worldwide, build swell models and access surf forecasts for all of the oceans in the world.

I remember my first surfing trip to Hawaii. I had just gotten out of high school in 1963 and went to a travel agent to purchase my airline ticket. She looked in the OAG, called United Airlines and made my reservation. She then hand-wrote my ticket after validating the ticket with her travel agency ID plate. I paid her cash, which was the normal settlement procedure at the time. Today, I simply visit Kayak.com (or any other travel search site) and query the lowest airfare consistent with my desired travel plans, book the flight and pay with a credit card. I then print out my own e-documents and boarding pass.

When I made my first surfing trip to the east coast, I only called my family once during the 10 weeks I was gone. I called them collect, and it was a very costly proposition indeed. I did send them post cards and letters during the trip though, and I remember receiving a hand-written letter from my father about everything that was happening at home with my family. I believe I still have that letter. Today, as I travel the world, I use my computer to call worldwide for virtually no cost whatsoever. I am in constant communication with my family via e-mail and our International cell phones. On a recent trip on a river cruise in the Netherlands, Using VoIP technology on my computer, I first spoke with my wife who was in Jeju, Korea and then my son, who was surfing north of Puerto Vallarta. We accepted this as the norm.

Computers and the Internet have changed all aspects of life. Yet, often times we are slow to pick up on the new opportunities that evolve with the changes. Surely, the changes may also affect us negatively as technology replaces what once required a skilled person to accomplish. But, understanding the changes and how they relate to the skill set one has is where opportunity is found.

Understanding the Paradigm

The Internet and World Wide Web have enabled consumers to research and consummate transactions in the most direct way. Unless there is tremendous value-added by an intermediary, consumer to supplier relationships will become more and more common as the web continues to evolve. Why? Direct connectivity represents the most profitable transaction for the supplier. It also potentially offers the best pricing for the consumer. Having layers of distribution intermediaries that add no real value other than marketing, documentation, settlement and/or delivery only adds to the cost for the consumer and detracts from the profitability for the supplier. Of course, there are many exceptions to this concept, but vertical integration is empowered by the Internet.

This isn't particularly good news for intermediaries, by the way, especially if you are not adding specific value to the transaction that the consumer (or supplier) is completely dependent upon. Just as travel agents were squeezed out of the airline ticket selling business by the airlines that vertically integrated into direct relationships with their customers, more and more service and product categories are evolving in the same fashion. Here are the reasons why.

Global Communication: While you may or may not use Voice over Internet Protocol (VoIP), it is now a very real alternative to using the telephone to communicate worldwide. Companies such as SKYPE (www.SKYPE.com) have revolutionized global telephone communications. Any SKYPE user can call any other SKYPE user for absolutely FREE anytime, anywhere. SKYPE is FREE to download and use. If a SKYPE user wants to make a telephone call to any landline anywhere in the world, he or she may do so for an impressive low rate (about 1.6 Euro cents per minute) As an example of the power of SKYPE, if you live in the U.S. or Canada, you can make unlimited calls to all Canadian and U.S. landlines for a measly $14.95 per year. Yes, I said $14.95 per year!
While VoIP had already empowered every person on the Earth that has access to broadband Internet and a computer to communicate worldwide, the future will only bring more affordable worldwide access.

Global Settlement: One of the biggest challenges that airlines had back in the 1960s and 1970s was the ability to document and settle passenger transactions. They relied upon travel agents to write tickets, receive payment and conclude transactions on their behalf. The payments travel agents received for airline ticket sales were processed through what was known as the "ATC Area Settlement Plan". This plan allowed for the distribution of monies amongst the various carriers that were involved in the transaction. The lead carrier was the plating carrier and therefore, would receive the entire ticket amount. Other carriers to the ticket would then invoice the "lead (validating) carrier" for the value of their ticket lift coupon for the segment (s) of flight (s) they provided. While this arrangement worked well, it put the down-line carriers in a very precarious position of having to provide the service to the passenger and then wait for the validating carrier to pay them based on the ticket lift coupons they had submitted. The ability to generate e-documents and directly settle transactions with passengers by using their credit cards is what led to the demise of the travel agency distribution system.

Today, even the smallest online marketer can settle transactions for minimum amounts by using the online settlement providers. Companies such as PayPal (www.PayPal.com) and 2CO (www.2CheckOut.com) have made it easy for all entrepreneurs on the web to offer settlement in every currency on Earth. Even online giant Google has introduced their global settlement platform. This is probably one of the largest advancements that have taken place on the web, and there are dozens of companies trying to enhance their services to replace the present lead of these companies. Global Settlement has empowered consumers to purchase services and products directly on a worldwide basis across virtually all currencies.

Global Keyword Search: When Google unveiled its search platform, it introduced the world to a whole new environment that continues to evolve. As the ability to search for specific results based on keywords becomes more and more refined, one can expect to simply enter specific keywords into a search engine and be presented with the optimum best website based on the keywords that were entered. As an example, if one were looking for a transfer from the airport in Buzios, Brazil to their hotel, by entering

"Buzios Brazil Airport Transfers" into Google, they are immediately presented with several solutions.

While at one time one would have gone to a Brazilian travel specialist and hoped that they would know enough about Buzios to arrange for transfers on his or her behalf, today the average consumer simply searches for solutions based on defining his or her request with the appropriate keywords. It doesn't really matter what you are looking for, if you enter descriptive keywords, it can be found through a Google search.

Google constantly crawls the web exploring page after page and determines what the dominant keywords are on each page. It looks at the links coming into the page and the keywords used for the link. It also determines the popularity of the page, as it relates to the page's top keywords. After thoroughly evaluating the page, Google assigns a "page rank" based on the pages relevance to the keywords. When the specific keywords are entered into a search engine, the page with the highest relevance ranking to those keywords is displayed in the number one slot delivered in response to the query. The page with the second highest page rank will appear in the number two slot, and so on.

This reality has ushered in an era of understanding how search engines rank web pages and the subsequent optimization of web pages to gain a high relevance ranking in the search engines. SEO, or Search Engine Optimization, is in part what this book is all about. The more pages you can create that rank high in the search engines for popular keyword search strings, the more money you are going to make. It is that simple.

Global Keyword Driven Contextual Advertising: Of course, Google isn't delivering free searches to millions of people just to be nice guys. Along with the free search results based on specific keywords, there are also "sponsored" results. A "sponsored" result is actually an advertisement that has been placed by an advertiser that has successfully bid on the specific search engine keywords. As an example, a local taxi cab driver in Buzios, Brazil may not have a web presence strong enough to gain top ranking in the search engines for the keywords "Buzios Brazil Airport Transfers". So, he or she may bid for those specific keywords in order that his or her advertisement appears as a "sponsored" ad every time the keywords are entered into the search engine. Because the taxi driver only pays the negotiated bid rate once a searcher actually clicks on his "sponsored" advertisement, contextual advertising has become extremely popular.

Contextual advertising has enabled millions of people to engage in commerce on the smallest scale but with rifle-like accuracy. Let's assume a 10-year old that resides on a small atoll in Micronesia has access to a computer and the Internet. He could conceivably collect shells during the day and offer them to interested shell collectors around the world by engaging in a contextual advertising campaign. The 10-year old could communicate either via e-mail or VoIP with his clients and settle transactions by using PayPal (or some other settlement product). This only leaves the actual delivery of the seashells to be considered.

Global On-Line Communities, The New Town Halls: Years ago, communities used to gather in the "town hall" to discuss matters of importance to the community. "Town hall meetings" were where folks would go to share their opinions. Today, there are hundreds of thousands of on-line forums covering every topic imaginable. There are undoubtedly forums for shell collectors, for visitors to Brazil (and probably one for visitors to Buzios) and for just about everything else. Where once a person might seek the advice of an expert on a subject, it is more than likely they now visit a forum on the subject where thousands of "experts" might be able to offer advice, experience and conversation regarding a specific topic.

As an example, I operated an on-line community at www.Cruise-Chat.com that consisted of over 15,000 avid cruisers. The community existed so that members could obtain the smallest detail about an upcoming cruise from other members that may have just debarked the ship or visited the port for which posters were inquiring. While no one expert could ever have the knowledge of 15,000 experienced cruisers, members wanting to tap the knowledge of the group, could easily do so. Further, because the intent of the on-line community was to help each other and no cruise line participated, the members believed they were getting the unbiased truth. Peer-to-peer online communities have become the focus of many consumers seeking advice before making purchases. The communities themselves have taken on a position advantageous to their members who rely on the experiences, ideas and knowledge of the combined membership.

Most recently, peer-to-peer social networks have gained extreme popularity and prove to be a major factor in the future as the first generation of peer-to-peer social networks shake-off their problem areas and become even more useful to their members.

The Travel Industry, Beneficiary of Global Commerce

As in the example of the 10-year old selling seashells globally, physical delivery of a product is still the main challenge of many business models. Here are some of the more important reasons that the travel industry, specifically, is an excellent place to focus your attention.

Travel and Tourism is a 7-Trillion Dollar Industry: Travel and tourism is one of the largest businesses in the world and is growing rapidly as nations of the world enjoy increasing economic freedom and success. While North Americans have enjoyed travel for decades, many countries are just now starting to enjoy mass-market travel.

Travel and Tourism Dominates the Web: Over 50% of all travel transactions in the world are taking place online for the first time in 2007. Airlines, hotels, car rental companies, resorts, cruises, tours, sightseeing attractions and other travel oriented services are increasing their web marketing and looking to maximize their online transactions as being the most profitable and efficient way to do business.

Travel and Tourism Does Not Have Delivery Challenges Associated With Hard Goods: Airlines use direct settlement and e-tickets and hotels use e-confirmations, as do car rental companies, tour guides, sightseeing attractions, etc. Even cruise lines are moving towards getting away from paper documents in favor of e-docs. The lack of delivery issues enables the worldwide distribution of travel products and services without facing the delivery challenge. Communication, conversion and settlement is followed by electronic fulfillment of the transaction.

Elimination of Intermediaries: While there will always be a need for travel professionals knowledgeable in niche markets to provide services in complex transactions, it appears obvious that even the smallest one-person operation offering a transfer service in a remote part of the world can communicate with potential clients directly and cost effectively. Clients looking for specific services in remote parts of the world can now locate and communicate with even the smallest supplier and get exactly what they want. No longer is worldwide communication a challenge or major expense. No longer is safe settlement across currencies a consideration and no longer is it necessary to have an intermediary between you and the supplier.

Creation of a New Fountain of Wealth: Travel and tourism is spending hundreds of millions of dollars to market its wares on the web. At one time, where there was simply no way to cash in on these expenditures unless you were national media, now you can cash in big time.

Travel and Tourism, The Opportunity: By understanding the nature of travel and tourism and the global distribution reality, you can easily identify opportunities to carve out your niche and start cashing in on the millions of dollars that are driving the online marketing of travel products and services. That is what this book is all about. By connecting consumers with suppliers and giving consumers enough information to make good purchasing decisions, you can easily become a content provider and tap the lucrative travel and tourism market. If you are ready to make some money, let's go!

Home
Based
Travel
Affilate

Chapter Two

Understanding Contextual Advertising

Years ago, my wife and I owned a Hawaii wholesale tour company named Windansea Vacations. We marketed a sophisticated Hawaii FIT product through travel agents in the 11 western states. Based in La Jolla, California, we did a good amount of advertising in the San Diego Union Tribune to drive business into the local travel agencies. We had signed a 1,000-column inch display-advertising contract and ran a 2-column by ten-inch ad in every Sunday Travel Section. At the time, the UT (as the paper is called here in San Diego) had a distribution of a little over one million readers. It was a very expensive process that had few guarantees, but we deemed it necessary to stay on top of the market. At the time, we were the dominant advertiser in the UT for the Hawaii category and, due to the advertising, became known as the Hawaii experts in San Diego.

I always wondered what would have happened if I had met with the folks at the UT and told them I wanted to continue advertising, but only wanted my ads to appear in those papers that were being delivered to people actually considering a Hawaii vacation on the day the paper was delivered. After all, delivering ads to hundreds of thousands of people that will never buy my tours seems kind of nuts. Then, to make it fair, I only wanted to pay for the ads that were delivered to that target group of subscribers that actually called, and I had a chance to sell them a vacation. I suspect they would have thrown me out of their offices, or worse, had me committed for insanity. As an advertiser, why shouldn't I have the right to qualify to whom my ads appear, and why shouldn't I only pay when the ad works and someone contacts me? It makes perfect business sense to me.

That is exactly how contextual advertising works and why it has enjoyed explosive growth with advertisers.

The History of Contextual Advertising

Formerly GoTo.com, Overture (www.Overture.com) launched its sponsored search service enabling advertisers to bid for search result placement based on keywords relevant to their businesses in June of 1998. Google then entered the search service market by introducing their AdWords program for advertisers in 2000. But, it wasn't until February 2002 that Google introduced its PPC (Pay Per Click) model, and that is what precipitated contextual advertising to become the giant that it is today. Realizing tremendous success with the AdWords program, Google created a program for publishers of content on the Internet that would allow these content rich private websites to also offer Google sponsored ads. Google's AdSense program was launched in early 2003 and introduced an entirely new business opportunity for content providers on the web. Yahoo subsequently acquired Overture in October of 2003 with the intention of competing with Google's AdWords and Adsense programs.

Today, Google still reigns as the king of contextual advertising, but Yahoo is hot on their trail with its own formidable contextual advertising program still in beta. While there are dozens of advertising networks to work with, by understanding what Google AdWords is and how it works in detail, we can see the advantages and opportunities of contextual advertising.

Google AdWords

Here is how Google defines their AdWords Program;

... Advertise to people searching on Google and on our advertising network.
... Reach people actively looking for information about your products or services online.
... Easily control costs – pay only when people click on your ad.

While this may be the understatement of the century, Google had indeed invented a better mousetrap. It is easy to sign up for Google's AdWords program. Simply visit Google and sign up. Once you have joined as an advertiser, your account will allow you to access a wealth of information on how to best run your advertising campaign for maximum effectiveness. There is an entire library of tutorials (both video and text) to walk you through every last detail of running a successful campaign. To get going, here are the steps.

Decide on Your Keywords: Running an AdWords campaign is pretty straightforward. You can visit http://adwords.google.com and sign up as a new advertiser. You should have a good idea about what keywords potential customers might use to find the specific product or information that you are offering. As an example, if you are selling a 14-night, 4-islands tour of Hawaii for $995.00 per person. You might want to run with the keywords "2 week, 4 Islands Hawaii Tour" or "Two Week, four Islands Escorted Hawaii Tour". The more specific the keywords, the more likely the Internet surfer will click on your ad. Your account at Google has some wonderful tools for selecting appropriate keywords. One tool will actually crawl through your site and suggest keywords that you might consider bidding on and another will run popular keywords that you might consider once you submit your primary keyword search string. Once you have determined your keywords, you would write your advertisement. Google allows you to use up to 12 characters in the title, 17 characters in each of the three lines of text and then a maximum of 35 characters in the link to your site. Google has a keyword suggestion tool on their website that will help you uncover popular keywords that you might want to use. Writing effective ads is one of the major challenges of contextual advertising. The Google ad for the Hawaii tour might look something like this:

Hawaii Tour
2 Weeks 4 Islands
Escorted for $995
Book it **NOW!**
http://www.2Week4IslandHawaiiTour.com

Establish Your Advertising Budget: Once you know your keywords, you can then find out the bid range for them. Google offers a tool for selecting your keyword strings. You simply insert your primary keyword search string and what you are willing to pay per click for the search string. It will then pull up all relevant search strings and let you know what the cost per click would be, as well as how your ad might rank with others that are bidding on the same keywords.

Using our 10-year old seashell salesman from Chapter 1 as an example, he may wish to only budget $2.00 per day and pay a maximum of $.10 per click. While this is certainly a low budget, AdWords would engage this campaign. The higher your bid rate for keywords, the more prominent placement your ad will achieve and hence, the higher the click-through rate on your ad because of its exposure. By using the keyword bid tool, you can focus in on those keyword search strings that will give you a high placement, but may be available for minimal click through rates. Google will track your ad performance for click through rates and help optimize your campaign with tools that understand how to best present your ads. The more successful (ie: the higher the click through rate) the less you will pay per click, so it behooves you to continually work on the effectiveness of both your keywords and your advertisements themselves.

Launch Your Campaign: Now that you have established your keywords, designed your ads, set your budget and click through cost, it is time to start managing your campaign. Your AdWords account will provide you with detailed information about your campaign, but there are a number of things that you can do to enhance the outcomes that you are after. You are obviously running the campaign to achieve specific results, and the more focused your results are the easier it will be to obtain them. Here are some ideas that you might want to incorporate into your campaign.

Optimize Your Landing Page: In our example of selling a 2-week, 4 islands tour of Hawaii, if your landing page is the home page of your travel agency website and not specific about the Hawaii tour, you stand a good chance of paying for a click, but losing the potential customer simply because he clicked for a specific reason. He followed the link on the advertisement to gain more information about that particular tour. If he has to wade through information irrelevant to his search or spend time looking for it, in all likelihood he won't waste the time. The link on your ad should lead to a page built specifically for the product or service for what the client is clicking to find. It should also have a way to complete the call to action with one click. Note that the ad we made for this tour had a call-to-action tag of "Book it NOW!" The sole function of the landing page would be to convert the visitor into a sale. By following the advertisement, they have already made a commitment to make a booking. So, now it is just a matter of convincing the visitor to book. There are a number of ways to do this. Make a special offer or incentive to book now, or stress how limited the opportunity is by implying there is going to be a price increase or that the tour is almost sold out. Offer an inclusion or value-added package of some sort to stimulate the booking or try other ways to bundle, offer or otherwise motivate the visitor to book. The call to action should only be one click away from the landing page, and any information that the visitor might need to make the decision to buy should be on pop-up pages that return the visitor to the booking form or landing page.

Use a "Throw-A-Way URL": Note that our advertisement shows a URL that is specific to the product being offered. This has a huge impact on the visitor's impression of the seriousness of your offer. With domain names costing on average a mere $8.95 per year, it is easy to justify using a separate domain name for each landing page. Just imagine how effective a landing page focused on the specific product that resides at a URL for the specific product will be. It will not only prove the commitment to the Hawaii Tour, it will also improve your click through rates on the advertisement.

Target Your Audience: By using Google's Regional and Local targeting, you can reach a local market when that is your focus. As an example, let's say that you are a cruise expert and want to reach every person that is looking for a cruise specialist within 25 miles of your front door. By running a local campaign, Google will identify every time someone within your geographical boundary uses your keywords to search for a cruise specialist. In this way, you only pay for clicks from people who are geographically viable for your services. For your local business, using Google's local search is an excellent way to find new customers that are within your geographical market but do not know that you exist. Once the potential customer has discovered the results of their local search, they can view your business location on a local map and print out directions to take them directly to your front door.

Another way that local marketing can benefit you greatly is by using it to market niche products and services to markets defined by zip codes or a geographical area. As an example, if you specialized in selling luxury products or services, you could focus your contextual advertising on those areas within the United States that are known for their affluent residents. By exploring the opportunities of using local marketing, one can target specific markets with rifle accuracy.

Site Specific Marketing: Another way to focus your marketing on high return opportunities is by using Google's "Advertise on This Site" functionality. I operate a website for home based travel agents located at www.HomeBasedTravelAgent.com and one of the resources on the site is a complete list of host travel agencies that have met certain requirements to be listed there. No one can buy their way on the list. I offer this to readers of the site so that they can have a list of potential hosts they can contact with some feeling of comfort that they are dealing with reputable host agencies. One day, I was looking at the list and noticed an ad that was served by Google that read "Tom Ogg Approved" as the headline. I went on to read the advertisement, which had clearly been written specifically for my site alone. The host agency had used Google's "Advertise on This Site" functionality to focus their advertisement to readers of the list. This was a very effective way to use contextual advertising.

Summary: Contextual advertising has revolutionized the connectivity between buyer and seller and has enabled even the smallest seller to connect with even the smallest buyer on a global basis. Contextual advertising has diverted billions of dollars from other forms of advertising and enabled global commerce on the largest (and smallest) scale. Launching an

AdWords campaign takes only minutes and your ads start appearing almost immediately. It is quite possible to launch an AdWords campaign and make your first sale within 15 minutes. Never before have such effective advertising possibilities been available.

Chapter Three
Understanding Advertiser Networks

When Google explains their AdWords product as "*Advertise to people searching on Google and on our advertising network*", what do they mean by "advertising network"?

We are all familiar with doing a keyword search on Google's far-reaching search engine and are also familiar with seeing the results of the search. Typically, one initially focuses on the free results that are listed in hierarchical order based on relevance to the keywords that were used to launch the search. The website that has the highest relevancy ranking to the keyword search is featured first. Then the second highest relevance ranking follows and then the third and so on for the thousands of results that it found with relevance to the keywords that were entered. One then notices there are usually two or three advertisements at the top of the page and more along the right hand side. These are the "sponsored" ads that have been created by advertisers using the Google AdWords advertising program and have bid for the specific keywords that were entered into Google's search engine. Understand that there is no charge for displaying the advertisements. The advertisers only pay their bid rate if someone actually clicks on the ad to visit their site (landing page). It is important to remember that ads served by Google in this environment are dependent upon the keywords entered into the search box on their search engine, and the ads are then served with the person paying the highest bid rate in the best position, and then the second, third and so on.

I am not sure who at Google conceived of the idea, but someone must have said something like, "Hey, wouldn't it be great if we could serve our AdWords sponsored ads on other websites?" Google was already expert at refining keywords and page content, therefore it seemed plausible they could devise a method of identifying what a page on the web was about and then serve ads that were relevant to the page's content?

It wasn't long after Google introduced their Google AdWords program that they launched Google AdSense. While Google AdWords is for advertisers that want to advertise, Google AdSense is for web (content) publishers that want to monetize their site by offering ads that are served by Google on their site. By monetize, I mean make a bunch of money by working with Google. Here is how it works. Let's say we have a page in our website about Crystal Cruises. By running AdSense code on the page, when a visitor views our Crystal Cruises page, Google will serve ads to that page that are relevant to the keywords "Crystal Cruises". As publisher of the site, we have complete control over the format and density of the ads. The ads may appear in many different ways, but if the visitor sees an ad that he or she would like to follow, you make money when they do so. How much money you make depends on the bid rate for the advertisement and to a lesser extent how well your website performs overall. The millions of websites that are running the Google AdSense program make up the Google "Advertiser Network". So, if you run a

Google AdWords campaign, your ads not only show up when the keywords that you have bid on are entered into Google's search engines, they will also show up on websites with a high degree of relevance to the same keywords.

Just exactly how much a publisher is paid is based on a formula that Google does not share with anyone. However, once you have signed up as an AdSense publisher, you can easily track your daily revenue. Google pays the publisher a percentage of the bid rate, and your revenue stream simply depends upon the total number of click-throughs that are generated from your website. When you visit your Google account, these are the things that you can track.

Page Views: Google tracks every page view that has the AdSense code on it. The number of page views that Google tracks is quite different than the page views that your metrics might show. The reason for this is that Google does not count anything but the real viewers (no spiders or robots) that are served ads. Some folks that use Firefox, as an example, may have blocked the ads. Google would not count these page views. Evolving content to stimulate an increase in page views is a strategy for increasing revenue.

Clicks: Google counts and tallies each and every click that is made by your visitors. The number of clicks is very important, because the more clicks you can motivate the more money you will make. If you have a static page view rate, increasing your clicks is another strategy for increasing your revenue.

Click-Through Rate: Next is the rate of clicks compared to the number of page views. A site's click-through rate is vital to profits. Later in this book, I am going to tell you how I made one simple change to the way I displayed my Google Adsense ads and increased my click-through rate by over 1% immediately. This one change meant another $1,200.00 per month income without lifting a finger.

CPM: CPM stands for Cost per Thousand (M) and has been the traditional way for publishers to charge advertisers on the Internet before PPC Contextual advertising. Your CPM rate is vital to your profitability and is quite manageable. This will be discussed in greater detail later in this book, but suffice it to say that increasing your CPM rate is critical to making more money with Google's Adsense program.

Amount Earned: Finally we come to the bottom line. The amount that you have earned serving Google's Adsense on your site is a function of page views, your click-through rate and CPM. This is a very manageable number and is something one can impact in a number of ways that will also be discussed in a subsequent chapter.

It's All About The Keywords

If you are starting to get the idea that keywords run the Internet, you are correct. Understanding the relationship between contextual advertising and specific keywords is critical to making tons of money as an affiliate. Here are some ideas I want to introduce now to start you thinking about how keywords can make you money.

Google Sees Every Page it Crawls as an Opportunity to Assign Specific Keyword Ranking: When Google visits a site, it follows every link that has been placed in the site and also follows all of the incoming links to the site. Google assigns the same weight to a page that may be three or four links deep from the site's home page as it does to the home page itself. In this way, each page within a website is evaluated solely on its own identity. Knowing this, it is quite likely that your most popular page to a search engine may well be a subordinate page in a website. To look at this fact another way, each page within your website is a specific opportunity for you to capture a different set of keywords within your web. The more keyword driven pages within your website, the more potential there is for visitors searching the Internet to find you. If you consider each page within your web as a potential keyword portal, then you can begin to understand the opportunity. Further, the more specific each page in your web relates to a precise keyword search term, the more relevant the advertisements will be that are delivered to the page, and when viewed by a potential visitor the higher the likelihood they will click on an ad. This results in a higher click-through rate. If the keywords were also chosen based on their bid rate, it will mean a higher CPM and a higher bottom line. Just as an elementary guideline of what Google specifically looks at when it crawls a page within your website, here is a list:

The Hyperlink to the Page: The first thing that Google reviews is the link to the page it is going to crawl. It looks for clues as to what the page is about and examines the link very carefully. As an example, let's say a web page is specifically about bone fishing in Cozumel, Mexico. There are several ways to link to the page (.../bf, .../BF,...Bone, ...Bn_Fs,.../BoneFishing and so on) Knowing that Google is looking for keyword links to begin to understand what keywords are relevant to the page, a good way to link to this page would be.../bone-fishing-Cozumel.html. This gives Google the idea that the page is going to be about bone fishing in Cozumel. The words are separated by a hyphen to let Google know that they are three separate words, rather than try to sort out all of the possible variables that may exist within the words such as one fish, etc. As another way to separate the words, I have also used underscores, such as .../bone_fishing_Cozumel.html with great success.

The META Tags: META tags are not as important as they once were considered, but are still an opportunity to let Google know what keywords the page is about. Here is how I would structure the META tags on a page about Bone Fishing in Cozumel, Mexico.

```
<head>
<meta http-equiv="Content-Type" content="text/html; charset=windows-1252">
<title>Bone Fishing Cozumel, Mexico</title>
<meta name="description" content="Bone Fishing Cozumel, Mexico Reservations and Information">
<meta name="keywords" content="Bone Fishing Cozumel Mexico (and then add other relevant keywords)">
</head>

<body>
```

Notice that the main keywords lead the way for the search engine to verify that the web page is about Bone Fishing Cozumel.

Throw-away URL: If this page were actually a landing page to convert PPC visitors into converted reservations (or other sale) then one might want to use the domain name www.Bone-Fishing-Cozumel.com to further enhance the keywords to a visiting search engine. I have been told that having the keyword URL adds about a 14% to 17% advantage in a keyword search. So, everything else being equal, the site with the keyword domain name (in this case www.Bone-Fishing-Cozumel.com) would expect to gain the number one position in search engines and also have extremely relevant ads served by Adsense.

The Page's H-1 Headline: This is extremely important. Many web developers use a graphic for the main page title. This is a huge mistake as Adsense assigns a heavy weight to the main title of the page. In this case we would want to run our H-1 headline using the keywords "Bone Fishing Cozumel" in 18 pt. Type. You can see that by structuring this page with the primary keywords repeated, it leaves little doubt as to what the page is about.

The Keyword Density in the First Paragraph: Also of keen importance is the density of the main keywords within the first paragraph. Google especially wants to confirm that the text is actually about the keywords and will seek out the exact density of those keywords, especially within the first paragraph.

The Entire Keyword Density on the Page: Once it establishes the main keywords, Google will crawl your entire page to validate that the keyword density is relevant to the keywords it has found so far. It will assess the most relevant keywords and start to assign a relevance ranking for the major keywords.

Links to the Page: Google will then crawl up every external link to the page on the entire Internet. It will identify what keywords were used to link to the page and it will determine each link page's popularity (known as page rank). Generally speaking, Google ranks page popularity quite high with regards to keyword search strings. If one page has a substantial number of links from high ranking pages, then Google assumes it is because the content on the page being linked to is superior to that of a less popular page.

Freshness of Content: Google also tries to determine how current the content is in a website by crawling its publishing logs. The reasoning behind it is that one is likely to find information found in today's newspaper more interesting than information found in a newspaper two-months old. Websites that continually update their content are viewed as much more desirable than those that do not.

Keyword Optimization and Making Money

While all of this may seem daunting at first blush, this is the language of making tons of money on the web. Keyword optimization allows you specific benefits that will pay you handsomely.

If Google (or other search engines) rank your page highly enough, you will enjoy numerous free visitors that have found you among the "free" search results in the search engine. This can be a huge bonus if the search engine starts ranking many of your optimized keyword pages in the number one, two or three position for the keywords that you are using on each page. Remember, that each page is another opportunity to control another keyword search string, and over time, you could be the beneficiary of thousands (tens of thousands in some cases) of free visitors daily. This traffic is going to drive a considerable amount of revenue from click-throughs.

Once your webpages are optimized for specific keyword search strings, Google will serve the most relevant advertisements based on your keywords. By serving extremely relevant ads, your click-through rate will increase dramatically. This should underscore the need for understanding the relationship between keyword search strings, search engines and PPC advertising. Your ability to identify profitable keyword search strings, then build web pages for the search string, attract traffic and maintain current content will lead you to profits you may have only imagined before now.

Chapter Four

Evolution of Travel Affiliate Marketing

Back when we had several travel agencies, I well remember one of the most effective ways to obtain new clients was to encourage our existing clients that were happy with our service to refer their friends and neighbors. Whenever we received such a referral, the new client came to us already sold on our service and anticipating the same kind of relationship that our agency shared with the person that referred them.

It was the single best way for our agencies to expand our client base. Client referrals were so desirable that we tried every incentive known to mankind to encourage them to occur. When a client referred customers to us on a recurring basis, we made sure to recognize their referral with gifts and recognition. I believe, in any business, third party referrals are the strongest kind of new customer.

Based on the testimonials of satisfied clients who have referred them, they already come to the business with the conviction that the business is viable, honest, effective and reputable. Often times, this third party is a close acquaintance of the person being referred, and other times, the referring party is simply a knowledgeable person who has an expertise in the market and in a position to make referrals. Of course, this all took place long before the Internet started to penetrate the travel industry.

As the web evolved, many travel suppliers embraced the opportunity to change their business models to favor a direct relationship with their customers. By offering direct settlement and e-documentation, they eliminated the need for an intermediary to process the transaction. As airlines, hotels and resorts, car rental firms and such moved towards vertical integration, one thing became crystal clear. They still needed the ability to drive traffic to their websites in order to serve their clients and fulfill their specific needs.

During this period of time, banner advertising was the primary method of attracting the attention of customers plying the web for information and services. Websites that had a readership of business people might well have been the target for an airline's banner ad in hopes of convincing the consumers that their airline was their best choice. While, initially, banner ads were interesting to consumers, ultimately, the proliferation of banner ads caused consumers to lose interest and become blind to them. While travel suppliers were still paying huge amounts of money to advertise, there was little that could be measured in terms of results. Eventually, banner advertising fell from favor, and as banner advertising CPM rates fell from their lofty highs, suppliers tended to abandon them as a viable marketing vehicle.

About the same time frame, Amazon.com was evolving their marketing model that included giving anyone with content on the Internet the ability to market books specific to their content on a revenue share basis. While Amazon.com did not invent affiliate marketing, it certainly launched the current version. Amazon.com believed if it could enable millions of websites to offer their books with relevant content, the subsequent referral of the customer to Amazon.com to conclude the purchase would be just as good as a third-party referral. Based on Amazon.com's subsequent success as the world's largest online bookstore, they were correct in their assessment of the power of affiliate marketing.

The Effect of Current Trends on Affiliate Marketing

One of the most common discussions that occur regarding online commerce is how consumers relate to supplier-direct commerce and the online environment. Many people take the position that complex leisure transactions will always require an intermediary, and while change will not happen overnight, here are considerations that indicate the direction of that change.

Dynamic Packaging: Still evolving, dynamic packaging promises the ability for a consumer to purchase dissimilar items from different suppliers and compile the components into one transaction. As an example, a person traveling to Hawaii on vacation may book a hotel on Oahu, a condo on Maui, their complete airfare, airport to hotel transfers in Honolulu and a rental car in Maui. They may shop for the best available pricing and confirm the entire itinerary in one transaction. Dynamic packaging will dramatically reduce the need for intermediaries in situations where they are present to consolidate travel elements into single transactions.

Online Communities Will Become the Intermediaries of the Future: Consumers researching complex leisure transactions will resource information from online communities that have evolved for the specific purpose of sharing information with its members. Online communities take on the same roll as client referrals did at one time and fit the Affiliate Marketing business model quite nicely.

Future Consumers Will Think Nothing of Buying Online: There are really three separate types of consumers that Affiliate Marketing affects and by identifying them, it is easy to understand why Affiliate Marketing will continue to increase in size and scope.

The Baby Boomers: Now the "mature" market, Baby Boomers are somewhat familiar with e-commerce. They have adapted to commodity type transactions because they had no recourse. However, most Baby Boomers would rather purchase complex travel events from someone with whom they trust and share a relationship. Most well-traveled Baby Boomers are active in community groups and have also taken to researching the elements of future travel plans online. While they may still purchase from an intermediary, by using the web, they have gained the knowledge to make sound purchases.

Generation X: Generation X made eBay what it is today. Raised on Game Boy, Nintendo, cell phones and personal computers, they think nothing of making purchases on the web and across global borders. Generation X is becoming the center of online commerce. They readily accept new technology and will think nothing of making complex, large dollar amount purchases online.

The Gamer Generation: Today's young adults were raised playing highly complex computer games, participating in social networks and interactive environments and have a complete "self" orientation. They are used to being in control and demand things instantly. The Gamer Generation will see a complete dismantling of intermediaries and accept the rise in global commerce as a natural progression of events.

Increasing Competition between Online Marketers: As more and more travel related products and services will vertically integrate into Affiliate Marketing in order to capture a huge growth opportunity, competition for key affiliate sites will increase, and the affiliates will be in a great position to profit from the competition. Bid rates for keywords to redirect traffic to supplier sites will increase, and competition between contextual advertisers to obtain affiliates for their programs will increase the affiliate's share of the bid rates. All in all, it is a very exciting proposition for affiliates that garner enough traffic on the web around high bid keywords.

Understanding Affiliate Marketing

Affiliate marketing is nothing more than an effective form of online advertising that works to everyone's advantage. The advertiser appoints an independent website as an affiliate. Then, the affiliate runs textual, graphical or other creatives to motivate their visitors to visit the advertiser's site to accomplish a certain task as defined in the Affiliate Agreement. Upon completion of the task, the advertiser pays the Affiliate an agreed upon sum of money. It is that simple.

Why Supplier Like It: Suppliers love Affiliate Marketing, as it gives them a chance to handpick their Affiliate websites and enter into a lucrative agreement with them. In all Affiliate Marketing programs, the supplier only pays when a specific agreed upon task is accomplished. If an affiliate does not perform, the supplier does not pay. It allows the supplier to closely control his or her marketing budget as it relates to results. Coined also as Pay for Performance Marketing, Affiliate Marketing is becoming the preferred choice of many online marketers of travel services and products. The key to understanding why suppliers rank Affiliate Marketing high on their list is simply this, Affiliate Marketing leads to a consumer direct sale with direct settlement with a known cost-per-sale for the acquisition of the sale itself. This customer to supplier connection promises the highest internal yield of any distribution channel.

Why Consumers Like It: Consumers like the process of controlling their own destiny when researching and consummating an online transaction. When consumers have a relationship with an affiliate's website, they tend to accept referrals as valid, thus making the affiliate a very productive way for consumers to seek out purchasing opportunities that are somewhat qualified. Online communities are the epitome of this type of affiliate/consumer relationship and generally offer the consumer the opportunity to validate their buying decision with the group.

Types of Affiliate Marketing Programs

While there are many different affiliate marketing programs and all of them seem to be somewhat different, there are basically three different affiliate models and each program will usually fall under one (or more).

Pay Per Click (PPC): A PPC format is pretty simple and easy to understand. The advertiser agrees to pay the publisher (affiliate) a fixed rate each and every time someone clicks on their link to visit the advertiser's site. Many advertisers will narrow the payment to new unique clicks and some will narrow it even further to simply new and unique to the advertiser's site. PPC advertising is losing some interest simply because, as consumers become more and more used to contextual and graphical advertising, the click through rates seem to drop. While this means less income to the affiliate, the advertiser still has maximum exposure from their creatives. However, a good PPC campaign can rack up an unbelievable amount of revenue in a short period of time for affiliates if they have a willing and active readership.

Pay Per Action (PPA): This model offers remuneration to the affiliate every time one of the affiliate's readers clicks on the advertiser's creative and completes a stated action. An example of this might be that a cruise line will pay x dollars every time someone clicks and then requests a price quote. Maybe another supplier is building a mailing list, and they would offer x dollars every time a non-subscriber clicks and then joins their e-newsletter list. PPA programs can be great sources of revenue as long as the program offers value to the consumer.

Pay Per Sale (PPS) or Revenue Share: This is the most vibrant of the three types of affiliate marketing programs and the one most often seen in the travel industry. Google's Adsense program is actually a revenue share format, as is Amazon.com's. No one makes any money until the consumer actually has an economic impact on the supplier. In the case of Google's Adsense, the consumer used advertising that is paid for by the Adwords advertiser, and the affiliate then participated in the revenue share of the bid rate. In the case of Amazon.com's program, the consumer purchased a book (or other product) and Amazon.com paid their affiliate a portion of the profits. Many travel suppliers offer Revenue Share opportunities to travel affiliates.

How Affiliate Marketing Programs Work

Initially, affiliate marketing fell on its face, as every Tom, Dick and Harry was using it for MLMs, pyramid schemes and other shaky business concepts. The software itself was unsophisticated and ineffective. Amazon.com spent millions developing their affiliate program and maturing the software category. Today, there are dozens of third party operators that offer turn-key affiliate marketing solutions to anyone wanting to use their services. It is quite simple to start an affiliate marketing program, but a little more difficult to recruit effective affiliates to market your products. Here is how it works:

Affiliate Marketing as a Supplier: Initially, you would contact one of the affiliate marketing software companies to set up your affiliate program. This will require you to define your objectives and detail your program. You would provide the textual, graphic or other link creatives that affiliates would use, your Affiliate Marketing Agreement and any other pertinent facets of your program. A good amount of thought must go into this process, but the company hosting your affiliate marketing program can help you through the procedure. The best results are achieved when you appoint an "Affiliate Manager" that will communicate and motivate affiliates to perform on your behalf. They should also monitor affiliates to make sure that they are operating within the guidelines of the Affiliate Agreement between the supplier and the affiliate. The company handling your program will take care of all of the operational details and provide you with a dashboard to your affiliate network so that you see exactly what each affiliate is doing, as well as the entire picture. The company will provide you with the payment information so that you can pay your affiliates in accord with your Affiliate Agreement. Basically, the Affiliate Marketing software company will handle all of the details of your affiliate marketing operation, thus reducing your job down to marketing the affiliate opportunity to potentially excellent affiliates to grow your business.

Affiliate Marketing as an Affiliate: When you make the decision to sign up as an affiliate with the supplier, you would visit their site and then click on the "affiliate" or "partner" hyperlink. This will actually direct you to the company that is operating the affiliate program for the supplier. They will ask information about how to make payments to you and specific information about your website(s). Once you submit your application, your site is usually visited by the supplier's Affiliate Manager to verify that it is consistent with content for which they are interested in placing advertising. Then, you would be contacted with an e-mail of acceptance and provided with the various creative link options for you to use on your site(s). You will also be provided with a link or access code to your personal dashboard that allows you to see exactly what is going on with your account. The dashboard information is usually updated in real time, so you can see exactly how many clicks have come from your site, how many sales have been consummated and, most importantly, how much money that you have made. When you have an affiliate program that is really productive, it is always fun to watch the dollars rack up while you seemingly do nothing at all.

It is important to understand that the third party affiliate marketing software company is the one operating the software and not the supplier. You can rely on the fact that what you are seeing is true and correct. Once you are armed with these numbers, you will want to start improving your site's ability to generate more income. This can be done by optimizing each page on which the affiliate-links reside, tracking the performance of the creatives and analyzing these results. We will get into this most important topic later in this book.

Home Based Travel Affilate

Chapter Five

Building Travel Affiliate Websites

While this book assumes that you are already competent at creating and building websites, this chapter will look at the specifics in creating winning websites that will perform beyond your wildest expectations. Much of the information contained in this chapter is quite subjective, and I wouldn't be surprised if some web guru or other Internet expert finds this information not consistent with their beliefs. In the final analysis, any new information that you receive will just be one more resource to help you along the way. I certainly do not have all the answers, nor does someone that will disagree with what I am about to share with you. All I can tell you is these tactics worked for me, and I believe that they are one direction to lead to the path of success. I fully intend to put a chat group on www.HomeBasedTravelAffiliate.com so that we can all share our experiences and insight to our mutual advantage. It is precisely this kind of sharing that will enable all of us to take full advantage of the opportunities at hand.

If I sound a little over sensitive to this subject, I am. I had a travel entrepreneur that kept calling me week after week tapping me for information on how to make money as a travel affiliate. Based on my personal success, I shared many concepts with her. However, she was more specific action-oriented and didn't seem to grasp the larger picture of evolving winning websites. The conversation finally came to a halt when, after a long conversation, she pointed to something that I had shared with her as being incorrect. While that may have been the case for her specific application, building a winning website results from understanding the overview and then experimenting, revising and refining until you discover what proves most effective. There is no cut and dry method that is the end-all for travel affiliate websites.

With that said, here are suggestions that I can offer that have worked for me in the past and are ideas that I use when planning and building a new web project. Many of the concepts introduced here will be discussed in subsequent chapters; so don't worry if some of the ideas seem like foreign concepts right now. The bottom line is to build websites with the focus of making money as a travel affiliate and no other reason. Succeeding will require you to test new ideas, evaluate them and continually work to improve the performance of your sites.

Design Your Site For Affiliate Advertising: This is the number one rule when you create a new website. Nothing is worse than adding affiliate ads after the fact. Trying to find where to place them on a page and in what size and configuration will lead to a disastrous result. Designing web pages that allocate the appropriate space for the placement of advertisements makes sense. Think about how magazines are laid out. The ads are placed in the prime locations first, and the content wraps around the ads. Your eyes are drawn to the ads, and the content keeps you flipping pages. This is how your web pages should work.

As mentioned in Chapter 2, Joanie and I ran weekly 20-column inch newspaper ads for our Hawaii tour company in the Sunday travel section. We quickly discovered there was a correlation between where the ad was placed and the amount of contact it created. We found that above-the-fold placement performed below the fold every-time. When the ad received placement on the right-hand corner above the fold, the results were even better. Finally, when our ad had the dominant typestyle and size and gained the aforementioned coveted position, it outperformed every other position in the travel section. Ads that appeared below the fold ads, on pages where the primary ad was a 2/3 page giant page-killer and resided in the lower left column achieved the worse results.

"Above the fold" in web-design terms means ads that are visible on the web page as it is opened in a browser. Clearly, ads that appear "below the fold" or require a visitor to scroll down for them to be seen are not as likely to stimulate a click through. When planning your web page, place all of your "above the fold" ads first and then worry about adding the content.

"Below the fold" ads are best used for specific purposes that appear to be logical conclusions to either one of the segments of the page or the entire page itself. "Closing ads" may offer the visitor the opportunity to further research the topic of the page by following related links (ads) and can be very effective. By designing your advertising space first and then the content, you can insure that you will not sacrifice your click- through rate due to poor ad delivery and/ or location. If you are using a web designer for the initial design of your website(s), make sure they give you the advertising layout before they start to work on the content and navigation elements of the design.

Forget Flash, Framesets, MySQL, PHP and ASP: This is really a very basic concept. Web designers love the latest technology. They love Flash intros and using frames to make sites really cool. They love database driven sites, such as PHP and ASP. In short, there is a wealth of technology available to really dazzle visitors. But, what do visitors really want? They want content, and they want it fast. If you deliver the content to them quickly, they will love your site. It is as simple as that. You will make money if visitors come to your site and then click on affiliate ads that appear there.

The way to deliver the most relevant affiliate ads is to have your web page optimized for the keywords that the content is about. Search engines love it when they can come to your site and immediately find your keywords, validate them and give your site a high relevancy ranking for the keywords. They do this by following the procedures as outlined earlier in this book. Adding anything that stands in the search engine's way of accomplishing this task is only going to be detrimental. My advice is to use basic HTML in either a tables laid out format or simple CSS. Using tables has the advantage of making sure that your ads will be delivered in a constant display, even though the content may change each time it is delivered based on computer resolution, screen size and format and the browser the viewer is using. CSS will give you complete control over the way the ads and content appear to the viewer, but may result in pages too large to be seen by viewers using lower resolutions or too small for a viewer using higher resolutions or wide screen monitors that are so popular with the Gamer Generation.

Use Textual Links: This is also very elementary. First of all, web designers want to dazzle you with great java rollover effects or graphical heat maps. Unfortunately, search engines can't see these, and you are losing a key opportunity to reinforce your keywords to a visiting search engine and/or ad server.

By using textual keyword hyperlinks, you are reinforcing your keywords (both in the text itself and in the link) to gain a higher relevancy ranking. Textual links load faster than any java, Flash or graphical link and visitors don't really care as long as the content is there.

More importantly, you do not want your visitor to differentiate between a textual navigational link and a textual affiliate marketing link. Think about it for a minute. If you are using a third party referral to drive business to an affiliate link, why make the link appear different than your navigational link? Clearly, textual affiliate links that mirror navigational links have the highest click through rate.

Use Descriptive Keyword Page Links: This is another basic concept. While we have already discussed it briefly, laying out your website requires evolving different keywords for each page of content in your website. The keyword textual link that you use should be named the specific search string keywords for which the page is optimized and should also appear in your H1 textual page title.

Use Alt Tags on Your Graphics: Be sure to use your keyword search string on no more than four of your .gifs, .pngs and .jpegs to reinforce the keywords to search engines. Since search engines cannot see graphics they eagerly look for the graphic's alt tag to find out what the graphic is all about. By using your keywords here, the search engine will pick up the information as part of its relevance ranking. However, be careful not to use the same keyword search string more than four times as the search engines may think you are trying to spam them, and it would have a disastrous effect on your relevance ranking.

Building Your Website(s)

While this book is about travel affiliate marketing and not a discussion of building websites, I am including some direction for those that are looking to acquire or enhance their web development skills. The time has long past when one needed to be trained in arcane code to develop a website. Today, anyone with even a minimal understanding of personal computers can create highly professional websites themselves. The only time one would need to go beyond what follows is if a highly technical website is being built, however that can be done relatively cost-effectively. Therefore, I have also included some suggestions on how to do that for a nominal amount of money in this chapter.

HTML Editors: The basic tool for web design is an HTML editor. HTML (Hyper Text Markup Language) is the code used to build basic websites, and CSS (Cascading Style Sheets) is a code that is used to set standards for HTML websites. Software stores are filled to the brim with web editing tools, and virtually all of them will perform the task. However, here are a few that will do the job best.

Microsoft Expression Web: Microsoft's current HTML editor, Expression Web is a great choice for people who use Microsoft products. Offering a familiar environment, most of the toolbars are the same as in other Microsoft products. Expression Web makes web layout a cinch and has taken CSS to a point where one needs no coding knowledge whatsoever. You can layout webs both in tables and CSS with Expression Web.

Macromedia Dreamweaver: Considered the standard for professional web designers, Dreamweaver has become easier to use with each new release. Dreamweaver will allow you to lay webs out in both tables and in CSS and is an excellent choice if you are a non-Microsoft oriented person.

Miscellaneous HTML Editors: A visit to any software store will reveal numerous web development tools, and, at this point, they are all viable alternatives to the two main products mentioned above. However, using industry standards is always preferable if you ever need to hire consultants or developers.

Other Web Development Tools: To create travel content (that usually means lots of pictures and graphics) you should possess the appropriate tools to prepare the various elements of your web content. HTML editors do a wonderful job of offering textual and graphical development, but here is a list of tools you will want to consider.

Adobe Photoshop: One of the most wonderful opportunities that exist for travel affiliates is to evolve web content using digital cameras and Photoshop. While digital cameras have evolved to 10 megapixels (and more), the subsequent sizes of the photos are huge. With Photoshop you can not only improve the quality of the photo making it look like a professional photograph, but you can also dramatically reduce the size of the photo by using Photoshop's "Save for the Web" tool. This will compress the photo into the smallest possible size so that it will load quickly on your site. It is quite possible to take an original photo that might be several megabytes and reduce it down to less than 10 kilobytes without losing any of the quality. This is a huge benefit for content that depends upon .jpegs for images. Remember, the key to your success is content that that is delivered fast.

Macromedia Fireworks: The only function of Fireworks is to create web graphics. Textual effects, static and animated banners, buttons, navigational structure and graphics are easy to create with Fireworks. This product should be in every travel affiliate's tool box.

Adobe Acrobat: If you are going to deliver .pdf content from your website, you will need to obtain Acrobat to distill the various files into .pdf format. While there are now a number of .pdf distillers on the market, Acrobat is going to give you the best of the best.

Using Web Templates

Web templates are pre-designed websites that one can purchase on-line from aggregators of web templates made by hundreds of designers.

Sites like www.TemplatMonster.com, www.TemplatesFactory.com and www.Pixelmill.com offer thousands of complete websites ready for you to load your content. For an unlimited source of web templates, just enter the keywords "Web Templates" or "Travel Web Templates" unto Google. They sell from anywhere between free to about $79.00 and can be simple one page designs to very complex 60-page websites. There are a good number of pre-designed travel templates to choose from and more are being evolved every day. The main advantage of using templates is that you can be up-and-running just as quickly as you would like. Templates are sold online and are usually available for immediate download and use.

Be aware that many templates are made to be HTML editor specific. As an example, if you are using FrontPage 2003 then you would want to search for "FrontPage 2003 Web Templates". So, when purchasing a web template, make sure it is compatible with whatever publishing software you are using. The one disadvantage of using templates is that they may have been sold to hundreds of other people for use on their websites. Many of the designers will modify an existing template to personalize it for your needs. Also, having a custom template designed and built for you is not out-of-the-question in terms of price.

Even though a template may only come with a fixed amount of pages, you can easily duplicate a page by saving it as another page. One trick that I use is to create an "A" page for each folder of a web site. An "A" page is simply a blank page that is ready for content and is optimized for the folder it resides within.

Finally, be sure that the template that you purchase can accept affiliate code and banners. If you are going to run AdSense above the fold, then you should be sure that the template could accept and display it. Of course, make sure that the template is also search engine friendly. Avoid Flash introductions, framed templates and other items that might intrude upon the website's ability to make search engines happy.

Working with Web Designers and Developers

While my advice would be to stick with HTML templates or simply designing your own websites, sometimes you may need to use a web designer/ developer to create a website for you. This would normally be the case if your site was going to be an e-commerce site, use databases, ASP or PHP or some other complex coding. Finding an honest and hard-working web developer can be a difficult undertaking. I actually had a developer quote me a price of over $10,000.00 to build a PHP site that I eventually had built, tested and loaded for $350.00 (www.CruiseTickers.com). I had another person quote me $8,500.00 plus a mandatory prepaid support package of 20 hours of support for another $1,500.00 to build a social networking site that I discovered was going to simply use phpFox. As you may or may not know, phpFox is a social networking (My Space clone) software solution in a box that costs $300.00 (www.phpfox.com)

The bottom line is that you need to do your homework before you commission any web developer to start on a project. Many times, there are existing scripts and code available that will accomplish exactly what you want. Once you are aware of the script, you can discuss the script modification costs rather than get fooled into thinking that the web developer is actually evolving the code him or herself.

Given my natural curiosity about technology, I started hanging out in PHP discussion groups and studying sites such as PHPBuddy.com, php.net and DevShed.com. I became more familiar with the capabilities of PHP and the realities of evolving PHP driven websites. That is when I stumbled across a world that I never knew existed. I discovered there are numerous programmers in countries all over the world that are looking for work and capable of doing a top-notch job for not a heck of a lot of money. But, how could I contact these developers and communicate with them?

Enter GetaCoder.com. I found several websites that connect website developers worldwide with those that want to have websites built. While GetaCoder.com is the site that I used, other sites that do pretty much the same thing are GetaFreeLancer.com, IfreeLance.com, RentaCoder.com and Elance.com. I am sure that there are many more.

Armed with a little knowledge of PHP and a very descriptive outline of what I wanted built, I signed up with GetaCoder.com and posted my job for bid. Within 12 hours, I had received over 20 bids from all over the world. One man in India bid a total of $350.00 to do the job and sent me a private e-mail with links to projects that he had done that used the exact technology that mine required. I was blown away by both his price and the quality of the work he had performed. I awarded the job to him. GetaCoder.com worked so well that I have developed a couple of other webs in the same fashion and with the same results.

Based on both my successes and failures in this process, I thought I would share some helpful tips I learned should you desire to have a website developed. While I was looking specifically for a PHP expert, bids can be made on all variations of websites and the cost is minimal. As an example, submitting a job for bid to GetaCoder.com is completely free, and you will only pay $3.00 when you award a job.

Know What You Want Before Bidding the Job: This is critical. You need to submit specific details of every aspect and component of the website that you want built. Include links to sites that are comparable in ways to how you want your site to look and function. Anticipate and include everything possible in your original description. Learn basic technology nomenclature so that your job description reads as if you are knowledgeable and expect a fair and honest price for quality work. Be aware that a poorly written job description will lead to problems down the road, so make sure to attend to this portion of the process thoroughly and with careful thought.

Understand that English is Likely the Web Developer's Second Language: Never use anything but correct business English. Many of the people bidding on your job live in countries where English is a second language and may be using a web translator to decipher your request. Never use slang, and avoid any use of words that might not be understood by the person with whom you are communicating.

Beware the Cheapest Bid: In an environment where labor is available for pennies on the dollar compared to having websites built within the U.S., always look towards reputation and past performance more than price alone.

Never Award Your Job to a Developer that is Not Established with the Bid Service you are Using: Getacoder.com allows buyers to rate their experience with the web developer. This is one way to insure that you will receive quality work on time. There are always newcomers that will bid on your job, but you are much better off awarding it to a developer that has dozens of satisfied customers that have posted their testimonials.

Always Use the Bid Service's Escrow Service: While shopping for coders globally is a fantastically wonderful evolution in global trade, be aware that there are people out there that will take your money and run. One of the things that I personally like about GetaCoder.com is their free escrow service. Here is how it works. You first deposit funds into your account.

When a job is awarded, the developer starts on the job. To prove that you are serious, you might deposit a small amount into the escrow account for the job. As the job progresses, you might deposit a little more. Once the job is finished, the developer will want you to deposit the full job amount into the escrow account before the job is delivered. At this point, you cannot reverse the deposit into escrow and the developer cannot access it. Once the job is delivered and you are happy with the results, you then release the money in escrow to the developer.

Hosting Your Website

Server space has become so inexpensive that it just doesn't make any sense not to buy the best that you can buy. There are basically three platforms that you can choose from: UNIX, Linux and Windows. While I have always used UNIX and been very happy with the performance, I now have one site on a Linux server and am equally satisfied. I have tried Windows servers and just don't care for the way they interface, but that is just my opinion. When you do purchase server space, look for VPS (Virtual Private Server) space rather than space that has restricted bandwidth and limits the number of domain names you can run on the server. You can currently purchase 4 Gb of VPS space for under $100 per month and you can host an unlimited (well, seemingly) amount of websites on the server.

While most servers come with an intuitive dashboard for managing the server, creating sub-directories, e-mail accounts and so on, I prefer the command line approach that UNIX offers as it gives one complete control over the server. It might take a tad longer to accomplish tasks at first, but the control will eventually be the feature that keeps you with UNIX.

In the company that may host your sites, look for how they are connected to the Internet. Most commercially viable servers are connected with a T-

3 line and also have a T-3 line backup. Support is critical and should be highly responsive. One time I was on a ship in the Greek Isles and found out that my main revenue site had crashed. I was able to get a signal on my cell phone outside of Santorini and called my host server support team who immediately reset Apache and got my site back up while I was still on the telephone. Support is critical to making tons of money. If your sites go down, you are out of business.

Home
Based
Travel
Affilate

Chapter Six

Content, Content, Content

More than anything, content is how you will make tons of money. The world of travel has so many unique opportunities to generate keyword driven content that it is difficult to even imagine an end to keywords and topics. Building lots of keyword-rich content is one of the necessary functions to cash in on affiliate marketing opportunities and one that is most important. Having page after page of keyword optimized quality content will allow search engines to locate your web pages based on the specific keyword search string that someone would use to find information about the topic of the keywords. Each content page within your web offers another chance for search engines to deliver traffic specific to the content on that page.

Of course, on the other side of the coin, when someone is conducting a search using the specific keywords for which your page is optimized, it will undoubtedly deliver an affiliate opportunity based on the same keywords. This will dramatically increase your click-through rate and generate an excellent income. Contextual advertising affiliate programs will also deliver advertisements based on the optimized keywords on the page thus offering another opportunity for increasing your click-through rate. All in all, affiliate marketing is all about evolving great content. Search engines want to offer quality content and consumers want to find it. As a publisher, you want to offer it to both.

What is "Quality Content"?

When folks use specific search words, terms and/or phrases, they are looking for thorough, complete and informative content. As an example, if someone uses the search term "surfing around Puerto Vallarta", they are probably looking for definitive information about where the surf spots are located and what the surf breaks are like. They would like to find as much information as possible as they may be planning a surf trip to Puerto Vallarta. If one visits the Puerto Vallarta Tourism Bureau's website and clicks on "Things to Do" and then on "Surfing", they find a page with one paragraph of generic text that doesn't really say anything other than there is surfing around Puerto Vallarta. This has wasted the viewer's time and is a prime example of a website not providing the quality content the viewer needs. However, if you had a website about visiting Puerto Vallarta with a specific content page about surfing, you would want it to include as much information as possible. It should provide authoritative information about the surf spots, locations, break descriptions, maps, pictures and anything else of relevance to the topic. Your goal should be to become the most accurate, definitive site on the web for information on surfing around Puerto Vallarta. By adding to the content as your site grows, it will become even that much more valuable to the users and the search engines. Eventually, with enough quality content, your "Surfing Puerto Vallarta" page could gain the first position in the search engines based on those keywords. Quality content is the key to driving traffic to your site.

When consumers think of quality content, they think of complete and thorough information on the keywords of their search. They have little tolerance for anything else at this point. They do not want to have to register, pay, disclose information or otherwise lose their anonymity to access the information. They also do not want to be bombarded by banner ads, pop-ups, page redirections or other tactics that interfere with their quest for information. However, links to pages that contain information regarding the specific keywords for which they are searching are very welcome. In fact, visitors will return to pages that have critical links for them to follow. Imagine that you are looking for information about surfing in Punta Mita; and you find a page that not only has complete and thorough content, but it also has 12 relevant links to information pertinent to the keywords. The visitors will probably bookmark the page and then return to follow each link.

Keys to Building Content

It Must Be Factual and Complete: While this seems like a given, one would be shocked at how many well-known sites offer faulty content. This often results when the information is done from research rather than personal knowledge. There are so many Internet "legends" that have been created by faulty research it is amazing. On a recent trip to Rio, one of the agents was adamant that Sugarloaf was on Corcovado. Having been to Rio several times, I knew that it wasn't and that they are two separate attractions. At dinner one night, she challenged me on my statement regarding Sugarloaf and then produced a report that she had printed in the Internet Café on the ship. The report was from one of the most respected providers of travel content on the Internet, and, sure enough, it reported that Sugarloaf was on Corcovado. Only after visiting the two sites while ported in Rio, did the lady finally relinquish her belief. Make sure that your facts are accurate by having them double and triple checked.

It Must Be Current: Nothing will turn visitors off faster than out-of-date content. As an example, if your site provided content regarding Cozumel, Mexico, it would need to have been up-dated immediately after the hurricane of a few years ago. Otherwise, you risked rapidly losing visitors quickly looking for current (and complete) information about what was open and what remained closed. Information on your webs should be updated frequently and represent the most current content of the subject.

It Must Be Accessible: No content should ever be more than three clicks away from visitor access. Having a broad site is much more preferable to having a deep one. Think of how to bypass unnecessary pages and have a clearly defined navigational structure. On one of my main sites, I used to have links to the major cruise line subdirectories on the home page and then send visitors to a secondary page for the balance of the cruise information. My thinking, at the time, was that it offered a second chance to get them to click on an ad. This is a mistake many Internet content publicists make.

One day, I decided to stick links to every subdirectory in the web complex "above the fold". My home page simply became links to all of the information in the complex of webs. Then, the content that had originally resided above the links I now placed below the links. Again, my original thinking was to have them read the information before presenting the links. The result? I had a 30% increase in traffic overnight as an immediate result of making this change. I got the message loud and clear. Don't make the same mistake I made in my initial design. Make your content available as quickly and efficiently as possible.

It Must Allow Visitors to Take Action: The reason that a visitor is exploring your content is to find answers. Once they have processed your content and evaluated your value proposition, they are ready to take action. They may want to keep looking for more information, they may be ready to commit or they may decide to eliminate the option. If they want to keep looking, your exit strategy should be to offer them the most viable alternatives to your value proposition. Why? Since the visitor has clearly decided not to buy now, by enabling them with the best alternative opportunities they will surely click on the advertisement that most attracts them. They will also leave thinking better of you than when they arrived at your site in the first place. While you did not make a sale based on your value proposition, you did make money via your exit strategy. Giving your visitors the best action conduits will enhance your value proposition, while at the same time, drive up your affiliate revenues. Since quality content is the key to making tons of money in affiliate marketing, the next question is how can it be developed?

Creating Your Web Content

Write it Yourself. Obviously, this would be the first choice to consider. Let's say you are an expert on golfing in Western Europe and have played several of the primary golf courses. Although this task may seem overwhelming at first, by taking one step at a time your website will grow exponentially. Begin the process by selecting one golf course and write a comprehensive review. The article should include as much information on that particular course as possible, as well as information on related ancillary data. In addition to your own first-hand experience, begin to compile information from outside sources. Contact the golf course directly and explain that you are featuring the course in your new website. Ask them to provide pictures, course information, maps and any other information that they have that would allow potential clients to select them on their next trip to Western Europe. Contact the Tourist Bureau in the country where the course is located and have them supply you tons of information regarding the area around the golf course. Contact the hotels that one might stay to play the course and ask for the same information about their property. I am sure you can see the process taking shape. By the time you have finished your article and review, you will have formidable content to offer folks looking for information about the specific golf course, and your expert opinion and advice will bring them back to explore all of the information. Of course, you have contextual advertising on each keyword page in the report. As an example, if the client is looking at a specific hotel's page, ads are being served about that specific hotel. I am sure you can see how this works. Once done with the first article and review, you move onto the second course and then the third and so on.

Never lose sight that the tourist industry worldwide exists to help you promote tourism to their country. Every hotel, resort, attraction, cruise line, tour operator, sightseeing company and more offer substantial tourism development tools that might consist of text, pictures, maps and graphics. Coordinate the use of this content along with your personalization and quality content is widely available.

You Can Use One of the Article Writing Tools: Let's say that you are not much of a writer, but have a substantial number of articles in mind. There are several tools that will research the web and offer articles based on keywords that you identify for the article. Once the raw article is created, you simply file off the rough edges, add an opening and a closing and make it yours. These tools are sophisticated, and creating articles and small e-book formats is a breeze. However, be aware that this type of content doesn't carry the same level of user satisfaction simply because it is not written from personal experience. I have provided a list of a few you may wish to consider.

InstantArticleGhostWriter.com: This is a great tool if you want to create a substantial number of articles. You could actually hire a high school or college student to start the process. Provide the various keywords for which you would like to create articles, then edit them when they have been created and generate hundreds of keyword driven articles. While not inexpensive, InstantArticleGhostWriter.com is quite effective.

Articlebot.com: Here is another tool that can create articles from keywords. It works by searching the Internet's various sites that use the keywords that are entered. It will compile sentences from the various sites and create an article that one can then make their own by modifying the text, adding an opening and closing sentence or paragraph and publishing. Once again, the quality of the finished product is not the same as one written from personal experience and many readers will depart with a feeling of doubt regarding the authenticity of the content because of the syntax and layout.

InstantArticleWizardPro.com: Here is another tool that does the same as the above tools. If your intent is to create a ton of content in a short period of time then this is another option for consideration.

WriteThatArticle.com: Still another in the pack of products that can generate a ton of articles for your websites.

While there are dozens more of similar tools, I think you get the idea. Just remember, quality is everything, and by using some of these tools, you may get quantity rather than quality. It is essentially up to you to hone these articles to make them yours and add the necessary quality.

Hiring People to Write Articles: Another viable way to get a volume of keyword specific content for your websites is to hire people to write your articles. While the cost is going to be higher than writing them yourself, you can hire a number of people at the same time to create a large volume of content in a short order of time. The travel industry is laden with travel writers who will generally work for a nominal amount of money. While the quality of their work is very professional, the opportunity to travel rather than monetary gain is often their primary motivator. Their writing income is used to offset the cost of travel and to create a business for which they can write-off these costs. A simple Google search using the keywords "Travel Writers" and "Travel Writers Associations" will disclose numerous resources for contacting travel writers to engage them. In addition to the aforementioned sources, here are some additional resources for content that you might consider.

iTravelSyndicate.com: This online marketplace for travel content allows editors of newspapers, magazines, websites and publishing companies to purchase nonexclusive, reprint rights for articles written by some of the best travel writers in the world. iTravelSyndicate offers its registered editors unprecedented flexibility and convenience at prices suited for even the smallest editorial budgets. Check out the site to see if their articles are of interest to you.

MediaKitty.com: This is a great site to contact travel writers worldwide. You can join MediaKitty.com for free and distribute requests for articles to be written.

CraigsList.org: I am sure everyone is familiar with CraigsList.org, but by using its Writing/Editing/Translation classified ads under the heading of "Services" you can post free requests for bids on articles that you want written.

International Freelance Sites: Today you can reach talent worldwide by using sites that specialize in reaching creative types around the world. GetaCoder.com, eLance.com, GetaFreelancer.com, Project4Hire.com, FreeLanceWriting.com, Guru.com and WorldPress.org are all excellent choices for finding reasonably priced freelance writers.

Using Other People's Content

Writing your own content or paying someone else to do it for you require time and money. Fortunately, there are several options in addition to those listed above. One of the ways folks market themselves is by writing articles for syndication. Many writers just want to have their articles published and read and are happy to let you publish their travel articles for free. Of course, the trick is finding the writers that want their articles published. But then, that is why you purchased this book.

There are tons of syndication sites that match writers with publishers. The best thing is that they do not charge anything for the service. You can access and publish thousands of high-quality articles by the simple task of registering at the various websites. Be aware that the author's by-line is always included in return for using the article. The by-line usually includes the author's name, a small bit of information about him or her and a link back to their primary website. Sometimes, the company providing the link will also want a link back to their site. This is a small price to pay for what could generate a huge amount of revenue for you. Below you will find a list of many of these syndication sites that offer tens of thousands of articles for your use.

Sites that Offer Travel Articles for Free

EzineArticles.com: This site has thousands of current articles on travel and leisure including tons of cruise specific articles. The catch with this site is that they limit the number of articles that can be used on each site to 25.

GoArticles.com: Here is a huge site with tons of travel oriented content. The articles are free to use, but you must include the author's bio and the articles may not be edited in any way. You will find lots of cruise articles here as well.

Articles.GetaCoder.com: This is a great resource with over 5,000 travel and leisure articles that you can use.

TravelArticleLibrary.com: Here is a travel specific site offering thousands of travel articles for free use. Once again, you must include the link back to the library and the author's bio and links.

Essortment.com: This site offers tons of great articles for the following niches: Us/Canada travel, European travel, Far Eastern travel, general travel tips and camping and backpacking.

TravelArticlesExpress.com: Here is another travel specific site offering tons of content for use on your website. The travel articles are broken down into numerous sub-categories making it very easy to find the perfect article.

Leonardo.com: This is an extremely interesting site. While it is much more than an article library, Leonardo's function is travel content management. The content providers are hotel chains worldwide, cruise lines, tourist bureaus and the like. It is completely free to register and download its content. Articles, pictures, video clips, maps and more are available for free use.

ValuableContent.com: This site has some quality articles, but also makes you use the articles with the embedded links for advertisements, which compete directly with your own affiliate ads. However, if you find articles that you want to use, your affiliate ads can be placed within the article in strong positions to overshadow the embedded links.

ArticleCity.com: This site offers thousands of travel articles on all topics that can be used liberally. However, the author's bio and link must remain with the article and nothing can be changed in the title or text.

Sites that Offer Travel Articles for a Fee:

PLRTravelArticles.com: This site offers a different concept. PLR stands for "Private Label Rights" so that you can use the articles provided by them and use your own name and contact information as if you were the original author. There is a $19.95 monthly cost associated with the service, but may be well worth it if you are branding yourself as a travel expert.

iTravelSyndicate.com: This site allows travel writers to submit articles that are for sale with non-exclusive reprint rights. As an editor, you can sift through all of the articles and chose the ones that fit your needs. Once you purchase the article, you may use it on your site forever.

If these are not enough for you, try a Google search using the keywords "Free Travel Articles" or "Free Travel Content". Remember, just putting a ton of travel articles on a website isn't going to produce much. They need to be organized around keywords and optimized so that the search engines can grant them high relevance ranking. If your site is about Bone Fishing in Cozumel, Mexico then the articles, pictures and other content should be about Bone Fishing in Cozumel, Mexico. You could have information about the various hotels, fishing boat operators, fish reports, weather reports, fishing tackle resources and so on. But, an article about anything not related to Bone Fishing in Cozumel, Mexico is more likely to hurt you than it is to help.

Finally, building hierarchal catalogs of articles is an excellent way to take advantage of the fact that all of the article sites are "search" driven in PHP. While the articles are excellent, they are much more usable when structured in a logical fashion and readers can view them in logical categories rather than try to search for them.

Home
Based
Travel
Affilate

Chapter Seven

The Power of Community

While we explored some sources for evolving content in the last chapter, this chapter will deal with the most wonderful opportunity that exists for website entrepreneurs today. To sum up the opportunity in two words: "User Content". User content refers to content that is created or submitted by those who use a site and is usually shared with the user "community".

Much has been said about "Web 2.0" and it has become the buzzword for every web marketer in the world. Loosely put, Web 2.0 refers to the evolution of the next generation of technology that has occurred since the bust of the web in 2001. The period of time prior to the debacle of the dot com crash is referred to as Web 1.0. The primary difference between these two web "eras" is their focus. In Web 1.0 the focus was on a business model that generated revenues from servicing B2B web needs. In other words, the focus was on solutions for major web players. Web 2.0 focuses on the empowerment of the "long tail" of the web, the millions and millions of small web users in the world. Web 2.0 entities are companies like

Google, eBay, CraigsList, MySpace and others that empower even the smallest web user with the ability to communicate, research, transact and interact globally.

One of the most important events to take place on the web is the evolution of peer-to-peer networks. Peer-to-Peer networks allow folks from around the world to converge to discuss and research topics of interest and generally become a part of an online community that promotes genuine relationships. Many community members derive a real feeling of belonging and acceptance. I, personally, have made life-long friends in online communities. Some I have never actually met face-to-face but still consider them close friends. Such is the online community world. What is important in this chapter for you to understand is the way that online communities can affect your online business and how you can manage them to make tons of money.

The Need to Connect

One of the obvious realities about mankind is the need to connect. Throughout history every culture has had their "community connection" where people became part of a bigger whole. It didn't matter if it was a camp fire, a church, a village lodge, a town hall, a capital or even a corporation, people need to connect with other like-minded people socially, professionally, romantically, educationally and in untold other ways. The Internet has ushered the concept of global community into existence in an almost bizarre way. Today, people from all points of the world share experiences, beliefs, opinions, knowledge, insights and every agenda known to man in online Usenet bulletin boards, forums, discussion groups and social networking environments. So strong are the devotions to online communities, some people have made them their primary social, professional and entertainment connection venues.

While this seems almost incredible, one only has to visit online communities to witness the actuality first-hand. Folks that are drawn to online communities are the same people that are also researching their next vacation on the web. Individuals comfortable in online communities are also comfortable with online commerce. As use of the web for commercial purposes continues to grow, so will the participation in online communities. Hence, it stands to reason that online communities are an excellent opportunity for growth.

Providing the opportunity for people to connect with other like minds and souls is one of the more challenging tasks of a web entrepreneur. Finding the right format to attract the groups of people that you want is as critical to a successful community as is the operation of the community itself. With well over twenty years of managing online communities, I am going to share what I have learned (usually the hard way) so that you can approach this opportunity well armed.

The very first thing that you need to consider is the scope of the community that you want to create. As an example, if you are going to organize a community for college students, you will certainly want to be completely familiar with social networks like MySpace.com or Facebook and focus on a specific niche using the same technology. On the other hand, if you are focusing on seniors that cruise, you will want to focus on technology that immediately empowers the individual without an invasion of their private information. In this instance, a bulletin board may be the best choice. Following are types of communities that you will want to investigate:

Usenet: Not actually a part of the web at all, Usenet has been a venue for global communication and discussion online for decades. Many people are unaware of Usenet because one needs to use a "News Reader" and subscribe to Usenet through their ISP. Many ISPs include Usenet with their access or you may use one of the many services that allow you to access "the News". By just Googling the keyword "Usenet" you will find a myriad of access points. Usenet is a global textual compilation of "Newsgroups" (same as bulletin boards) with every topic under the sun being discussed. One can easily launch a "newsgroup" on Usenet and publicize it for new members. Usenet is set-up in a structured directory, so finding what you want to discuss is normally easy. While Usenet is quite interesting, I wouldn't recommend it for starting a travel related community.

Bulletin Boards: A bulletin board is a discussion community that exists for the primary purpose of allowing members to discuss the topics of the various forums that exist within the bulletin board. A forum is a separate topic area within the board. As an example, one bulletin board that I created (and subsequently sold) is Cruise-Chat.com. While Cruise-Chat.com is a bulletin board about cruising, it was made up of several "forums". One forum was Royal Caribbean and was specifically for the discussion of topics related to Royal Caribbean Cruise Line. Another forum was Europe Ports and it was for the specific discussion of the ports in Europe. Members post messages, and the subsequent replies from other members are contributed to help the community. The messages are compiled into "Threads", or a logical display, that shares the information posted as if it were an ongoing conversation.

Bulletin boards are a primary community tool and the best option for your first entrepreneurial ventures into the world of online communities. There are a ton of bulletin board solutions with more being made available every day. There are many open source (aka free) bulletin boards to chose from, but be wary. If your community becomes successful, you may have tens of thousands of members accessing tens of thousands of page views daily. Further, there may well be hundreds of posts to the bulletin board daily. Unless you are a computer wiz kid and understand the subtleties of PHP, MySQL and other arcane programming languages, you are better off using a paid service that will host your bulletin board and offer support when something goes wrong (and it will). The most popular open source bulletin board is phpbb (www.phpbb.com) Many web designers can use this open source code to create unique and highly powerful, yet stable, bulletin board environments.

Before launching your new bulletin board, you should already have the nucleus of a community that can start using it. Nothing is worse than to launch a bulletin board with no active posts. A visitor will immediately move on if they see no activity or even worse, stale activity. Also, avoid the mistake just about everyone makes. Do not open your bulletin board with a ton of forums thinking that the more forums you offer, the more likely people will be to post. Actually, just the opposite occurs. A visitor seeing numerous forums with little or no activity will not stick around either. You are much better off having just one forum that has multiple daily posts than having 40 forums with occasional entries. Especially critical is making sure that every post gets a response. When a visitor first arrives at your community, they try to discern the personality of the forums which they base on user interaction. When every post receives at least one response, they perceive the community to be viable and active and will be less fearful of posting. Bulletin boards are a great choice for websites that focus on one aspect of travel, as the ensuing conversations will further refine the information that resides on your site.

Digests: A digest differs from a bulletin board in that members communicate with one another, but the posted messages are sent to every member in a digest format. Remember reading Reader's Digest? There was a table of contents that had each of the articles that appeared in the publication, and one could simply examine the table of contents and read those articles of interest. A digest does just exactly the same thing.

All of the conversation for the day is compiled into a "digest" with the subject titles listed at the top and the underlying articles further down the page.

Digests are powerful because the entire conversation is delivered to each and every member. So, rather than wait for members to come to your bulletin board, you take the conversation to your members. Digests are excellent for professional groups and those communities with close affinity. But, one should be cautious with a digest as it empowers many of its members in a way that they may circumnavigate around your specific objective. I once started a global digest for cruise agents with the intention of getting cruise professionals around the world talking and sharing information with one another. The benefits for the members were obvious. If an agent in California had a client cruising to New Zealand, a cruise agent in New Zealand was in a perfect position to help the one in California and so on. There was no cost to join, but members had to agree that CAD (as it became known) was strictly a vehicle to share information and help one another. No commercial activity was to take place. Thousands of cruise agents from all parts of the world joined and it became an immediate success. Unfortunately, its success spawned a second wave of unscrupulous members that violated CAD in every way. They were using it for their own self-promotion and there was even one unprincipled individual that copied the concept and tried to pass his clone off as the original. Given it didn't accomplish the objective that I was pursuing, I sold the digest to a travel industry association, and it is still operating today under a different name. Do use a digest if you can clearly state your objective and measure its success or failure.

Social Networking: While I have not operated a social network, I have explored the opportunity to do so. I had a perfect application for one and have spent months understanding how they work, why people like them and what it would cost to operate one effectively. Let me cut to the chase. I decided against it simply because I didn't think I could get one to work. Here is the challenge. Social Networks require a huge amount of server space and constant maintenance to keep working. The initial cost is minimal, as you can visit www.phpfox.com and purchase a MySpace.com clone for about $300.00. The challenge becomes having the software work consistently and what you will do when it doesn't. Further, social networking requires a certain "branding" of the nomenclature to fit the members as they evolve. This is one of the most difficult things to accomplish, as an error in nomenclature will cost you dearly. To discover your options (which are many), if you want to evolve a social networking site, simply enter the keywords "social networking software" or "social networking hosts" into Google. I suspect that we will see companies offering social networking sites with an easy barrier to entry and inexpensive monthly disbursement. After all, this technology is driven by the reduced cost of server space and the increased efficiency of coding on the Internet.

Advertising on community sites like those mentioned above is a very difficult task. Historically, click through rates are the lowest on discussion boards because of their nature. About the best advice that I can offer is to put your advertising prominently above the fold. Another great place to run ads is by the buttons that are used to navigate the discussion group. If you insert ads into the discussion itself, you will find that the members will complain, find it offensive and may even choose to abandon the site.

How to Manage Your Community

Now that you have your Usenet group, bulletin board, digest or social networking site, how do you manage it? This is one of the places where your investment in this book is going to pay off. Following are not recommendations but hard and fast rules that you need to live by when operating an online community:

Rule #1: When You Think Something is Wrong, It Is: No one can see the future, but when you think something doesn't makes sense to you, then take action immediately. The member posting the off-kilter messages may well have an agenda that is not in your best interest.

Rule #2: Set Community Standards and Enforce Them: Define exactly the purpose for the community and set specific standards. As an example, No flaming other members, no use of vulgar language, no soliciting, etc. When someone violates the community standards, they are sanctioned. If they continue to violate the community standards, they are banned.

Rule #3: Never, Never, Never Lose Your Temper: No matter how outrageous someone's posts become, always handle yourself in a professional manner. Remember, you are operating a community to make money and any breach in your professionalism will cost you dearly. Also remember, as the Administrator you set the tempo for the entire community. One outburst from you sends a clear message to the community that it is OK to lose tempers.

Rule #4: Never, Never, Never Get Into an Argument Online: Once again, unless you want a community where everyone is arguing, never break this rule. If you have a conflict with someone, take it offline and in private.

Rule #5: Be Fair to a Fault, but When it Comes Time To Take Action, Be Swift and Decisive. When someone steps over the line, give him or her another chance, but explain what the community expects. If he or she does it again, ban them immediately and don't look back. Once you have made your decision, stick to it without further discussion.

I hope these rules help you succeed with your own community. While they seem obvious, you will be amazed at how convoluted situations can become. Many times problem makers are very adept at arguing their point and may be able to twist things to make it sound as if you are the one that is off-kilter. Just pull out these five rules and abide by them, and you will be amazed at how effectively you can resolve conflict successfully.

Recruiting Moderators: A moderator is a community member that helps with one or more forums. They engage community members that post messages and comments and generally respond to many of the conversations. In part, their function is to stimulate conversation, but a large part of the moderators' role is to enforce community standards. If your community is successful, there is no way that you can be aware of all posts and conversations. However, forum moderators are generally involved with their forum(s) at a level where they are aware. By giving your moderators the power to edit, delete and ban users, they can effectively keep the forum(s) on track.

The best way to recruit moderators is by following members that post frequently and finding the ones that have leadership qualities. They are knowledgeable about the forum topic(s), they are well liked by other community members, they present themselves well in a written format, and they are never involved in confrontations, flaming, arguments or otherwise violating any of the five rules.

Once you have identified a person you would like to approach to be a moderator, do so with complete respect. Let them know that you truly value their contribution to the community, and you would like to elevate them to the position of forum leader. When approached like this, virtually everyone you solicit will accept. Since they are already active in a community forum, their role really doesn't change other than they are now recognized as a forum leader. Their additional powers of editing, deleting and banning posts and members gives them the ability to really fine tune the forum and they will take a great amount of pride in their efforts. Never offer payment for a forum moderator. Sites that pay their moderators lose the feeling of openness and honesty. The moderators become clear operatives of the community, and their objectivity becomes askew to a point where they become less effective, rather than more valuable.

Other Kinds of Community Content

While discussion groups make up the bulk of community content, there are several other ways to evolve content from your community.

Community Archives: If you have a successful discussion group that is churning out hundreds of posts a day on various travel topics, you can easily mine past threads and develop a thorough synopsis of each thread and present the information in a searchable or hierarchal database. You can create thousands of pages in your community archives that are keyword optimized and that also feature keyword affiliate messages. Community archives are wonderful tools for compiling a huge amount of content in short order.

Community Review Sites: If your community is discussing any aspect of travel, you can easily start a review site where community members can submit reviews of their own experiences. I built a cruise review site that turned into thousand and thousands of keyword-optimized pages that served Google AdSense ads and generated a 5-figures monthly income from Google AdSense alone. People want to share, and others want to read about the ship, hotel, port, restaurant, sightseeing event and so on. These peer-to-peer review sites are becoming the town halls of tomorrow and are a natural adjunct to discussion groups. As with discussion groups, one needs to clearly define the specific objective of the review site and set specific standards. As one can imagine, the standards for a luxury cruise site would be quite different than the standards for a European youth hostel review site. Be sure to match your standards with the community members that will be submitting reviews.

Community Projects: Have your community contribute content to a monthly e-zine, e-book, dictionary, and library of articles or any other means of compiling content for use either inside or outside of the community. By using Wiki technology, one can establish a community purpose and allow for a collaborative community effort to effect results. The bottom line is a community effort can create a substantial amount of content that can all be imbedded with affiliate advertising.

As you can see, user generated content is the best possible solution for creating a lot of valuable keyword-optimized content that can spin-off thousands of dollars in affiliate revenue monthly.

Home
Based
Travel
Affilate

Chapter Eight

Google's AdSense, Start Your Money Machine

Before we go exploring the myriad of travel affiliate programs out there, we will focus on the one that should be your first to implement. With Google AdSense, you will make money within 15-minutes of loading the code onto your website(s). If your website generates a modicum of traffic, I guarantee it. AdSense is a revenue share model in which Google will share the PPC rates that they charge for Google AdWords campaigns. Let us say that supplier "A" is running an AdWords campaign for the keywords "Eastern Mediterranean Cruises" and is paying $2.00 per click.

By signing up for Google's advertising network of publishers, you can insert code to pages on your website that will deliver the AdWords advertisements to those pages. Google will crawl each page and determine the most relevant keywords for each page, and when a user views a page, Google will deliver the most relevant ads to the page. If a page on your website is optimized for the keywords "Eastern Mediterranean Cruises", then it is quite likely that the advertiser's ad will appear on the page. If the user clicks on the ad to find out more information and visits the advertiser's website, Google will collect the $2.00 PPC rate from the advertiser and then share part of it with you. While no one knows the exact formula, just for the sake of an example, let's say that Google pays you 40% of the click through rate they collected; you would have made $.80 from the transaction. While $.80 doesn't sound like much, imagine if you were averaging hundreds of click-throughs a day.

As we discussed in chapter 3, advertising networks have a very specific role in your overall affiliate advertising plan. Having had years of successful experience with Google's AdSense program, I will share with you what I have found to be the most successful ways to make the most money. Of course, all of this is from my personal experience learned by trial and error, so there may be more information out there that goes beyond this discussion. However, I must tell you, I would have paid thousands of dollars for what I am about to share. I would have eagerly done so, as I would have made much more money during my learning curve that could have easily paid for the expense many times over.

The AdSense Code

After your sign up and subsequently accepted by Google as an AdSense publisher, you will be given a unique affiliate number and access to your own control panel which acts as an interface with the AdSense program. You are provided with reports on activity that you can customize, tutorials, video training and tons of help understanding how it all works. Next, there is an "AdSense Setup" tab where you will generate the code for your website. Note that there are three ways to make money with Adsense.

Adsense for Content: This generates the code that places the AdSense ads on your page. There are several ad sizes and shapes, known as "units", from which to choose. You can specify what kinds of ads that you want to appear on your site. I always use "text only" ads as they seem to look the best on the types of pages on which I insert the advertising. You can also select "text and image" ads, and this will allow Google to deliver both textual and image ads to your site. An image ad is basically a banner ad and may take up the entire ad unit. Your third choice would be to place "image only" ads on your page. Many times the image ads pay a CPM rate rather than a PPC rate and may be a good choice for sites with low click through rates. Note that the Google publisher's agreement limits you to placing a maximum of three ad units on a web page. Now, you can use any size ad unit and any blend of textual and image ads within the three units.

There is also a content selection known as a "Link Unit". A link unit is just that. It will suggest keywords that when clicked upon will then offer a good number of AdSense textual advertisements. These are handy little advertisements that can be used in various ways that we will discuss later. You can use one Link Unit in addition to the three Ad Units on each page.

AdSense for Search: By inserting AdSense for Search code on your site, you insert a Google search box on the page. Then, if a visitor uses it to search and clicks on a sponsored ad, you receive a portion of the PPC rate the advertiser paid for the ad. While the Google Search box is a handy way to make a few extra bucks, I have never found it to be all that profitable. Many visitors already have a Google search box installed on their browser and tend to use that instead. However, if you have content that naturally invites searches, it might be an excellent inclusion. You can install one search box per page in your website.

Referrals: Google understands Internet marketing like no one else and offers affiliates the chance to earn money by referring visitors to their various products. Referrals are paid to affiliates on the following products offered by Google: AdSense, AdWords, CheckOut (Google's new global settlement product) Google Aps, Firefox plus Google Toolbar and Google Pac (a collection of essential software). I place the AdSense referral link on some of my pages and make excellent money from its use. However, the pages need to be targeted to conversations that are relevant to the link. In addition to the above Ad Units, Link Unit and search box, you can have two referral links per page (any two products are fine and they can be different on each page).

Creating the AdSense Code

When I first installed AdSense on my sites, I went with the normal 468 x 90 banner ad format. I chose a color scheme that went with the web's colors and posted it right where a banner ad should be, at the top of the page in the center. I was happy with the initial results but kept thinking that it just looked too much like a typical banner ad one would see all over the Internet. I read every word on the Google AdSense site about how to make the ads work better and studied the "heat map" Google offered as to ad placement. I tried a number of different things to boost my click through rate. But, no matter what colors I used, it didn't change any more than a minute percentage. Then, one night when I was lying in bed trying to sleep, it came to me. People were becoming immune to the typical banner ads. Even though the banners were offering textual keyword ads, they still looked like banner ads.

I started trying different ideas and would monitor and record the results. One day, I tried something that increased my click-through rate dramatically. I converted all of the pages in my sites to this new format. Overnight, my click-through rate jumped by over 1 full per cent which, at the time, equated to about $120.00 per day! This was a huge breakthrough, as there was no significant change in traffic to explain it.

What I am going to share with you is well worth the cost of this book one hundred fold. If you use these ideas in your advertising, I guarantee you that you will increase your income from the very first day.

The More Your Ads Look Like Links, the Higher the Click-Through Rate: We are so conditioned to think that advertising must look like advertising that we fall into a familiar trap. By using a standard banner with borders and everything else to make the ads look like ads, I convinced my readers not to read them. The Google agreement doesn't allow you to manipulate the code for the ads. However, when you select the ad sizes and color scheme, there is no reason not to dump the borders by selecting the same color for the border as the background of the web page on which the ads are going to appear. This has the same effect as removing the border entirely. Without the border present, the ads look much more interesting and accessible and less like an advertisement.

Use the Same Font on Your Web Page and In Your Ads: Make the ads look like they belong on the page on which they appear. Using the same font style and size allows the contextual ads without borders to appear as if they are part of the page rather than a separate ad.

Use the Same Font, Size and Color for the Hyperlink in the Ad, as You Use for Hyperlinks On Your Web Page: Make the hyperlink in each advertisement look like another link on your page. Visitors are comfortable clicking on links that redirect them to other locations within your website. Therefore, they will think nothing is unusual about an ad that offers links that are identical to the links on your site. This is especially true when using Link Units. I have had great success using Link Units in the 5-ad horizontal format and displaying them in what looks like navigational structure. Check out www.HawaiiReviews.com and scroll down to the bottom of the page. Notice how the Link Units appear to be native navigation for the website. The more that you can make the advertising hyperlinks look like native hyperlinks, the more likely visitors are to click on them.

Place the Ads Where Visitors Are Sure to See Them: I have had wonderful success placing ads (designed as above) within the text portion of a page on the right hand side of the page. Everyone that reads the text automatically continues to the content in the ad that appears on the same line. The natural flow while reading text is from left to right, and the human eye cannot help but follow the text. However, if there were a border around the advertisement, the eye would normally stop at the border, as it recognizes that as being the end of the text.

Use Unique Ad Sizes: I had great success with the 336 x 280 large rectangle size, as when placed properly, it looked as if it were a text block with highlights of the surrounding content. It also appeared to be a sidebar worth reading and resembled nothing like an advertisement. Further, because the ads that are served are so relevant to the content in the article, this extra exposure has a huge impact on the click-through rate.

Installing the AdSense Code

Installing the AdSense code is really very easy. One simply configures the code by using the design tools provided on the AdSense site. When the ad unit looks the way you want, simply copy the entire code from the box on the AdSense site, paste it into the code of your web page where you want it to appear and publish the site. The first time that you load the page it is likely that it will not serve relevant ads, because Google first needs to crawl your page and determine the most relevant keywords before it starts serving relevant contextual ads. Of course, this is a very simplistic look at installing the code.

One of the features of FrontPage 2003 that is not offered in Expression Web (at this time) is the "Included Page" web component. If you are going to play the content game and want to make your life easy, get a copy of FrontPage 2003 and familiarize yourself with the "Includes Content" web component. Simply put, here is how it works: One creates a blank web page and then enters the AdSense code on the blank page giving it a unique name.

At this point, one simply needs to go to a page in his or her website and click on >insert >web component >Includes Content >page (browse to the unique page) and hit enter. Voilà, the code that exists on the unique page magically appears on the page. This is a great way to design your AdSense ads. Let's say that you have built 5,000 pages of content, and you want to change one of the ads. You can simply open the page on which the ad appears, change the code and then publish it. The ad will be changed on all 5,000 pages instantly. This makes managing your advertising quite convenient. This also allows you to experiment with different ad styles, sizes and formats and track the results immediately. Just imagine, what a monumental task it would be if you had to chase down the AdSense code on each and every page of the 5,000 individual pages.

Optimizing Web Pages for AdSense Code

One of the most important factors to making tons of money is your click-through CPM and rate. Nothing will improve this more than by showing extremely relevant ads to a page's keywords and keywords that are in high demand. As an example, let's say that one keyword phrase is bid at $8.00 PPC and another keyword phrase is bid at $.05 PPC. It is obvious that it would take 160 clicks on the low bid keywords to equal one click on the higher bid keyword phrase. By focusing on higher yielding keyword phrases, you can dramatically increase your CPM. By optimizing the keywords on a web page, you can dramatically improve the relevancy of the ads that Google will serve to your page. This is the secret to making tons of money.

By checking keyword search strings with Google AdWords and finding their bid range, you can determine the PPC bid rate and what its opportunity to generate a meaningful revenue stream will be. As an example, "Crystal Cruises" may have an $8.00 PPC bid rate while "Luxurious Cruise" might have a very low bid rate. If you are featuring an article on "Luxurious Cruises" you might want to rewrite the article slightly to accommodate the keywords "Crystal Cruises". As long as the intent of the article is not compromised, by making this small change in content, you should be able to significantly increase the click through CPM. While the content may have changed only slightly in the article, you can make a major impact on the ads by optimizing the page around the keywords "Crystal Cruises". Once again, it doesn't make any sense to optimize a page if the content doesn't jive with the keyword optimization. Here are some elements I have had excellent luck with when optimizing a page to serve Google AdSense advertisements.

Links to the Page: Always use keyword textual links to the page. Don't use Java, DHTML or any other non-textual link. In the case of the above article, I would use a link something like, "Crystal Cruises, Luxury at Sea". Always lead with the search string on links to the page.

Page URL: The URL of the page is also very important. Always separate all of the keywords with either a hyphen or underscore so that Google (or whoever is crawling the page) will see the words as separate words rather than trying to separate them when they are organized as one long string of characters. In the case of the above page, I would save it as "Crystal_Cruises_Luxury_at_Sea.html" or I might simply save it as "Crystal_Cruises.html".

META Tags: While not what they once were, I would insert the following META tags on the page:

<head>
<title>Crystal Cruises</title>
<meta name="keywords" content=Crystal Cruises Luxury Cruising at Sea ">
<meta name="description" content="Crystal Cruises luxury cruising serenade symphony (more relevant keywords)">
</head>

H-1 Headline: In 18 point type at the top center position on the page, I would use the textual title "Crystal Cruises" and a 14 point subtitle "Luxury at Sea".

Crystal Cruises

Luxury at Sea

Alt Tag: If I had used a picture or graphic on the page (say a picture of one of Crystal's ships or their logo) I would use "Crystal Cruises" as the alt tag.

Keyword Density: Finally, when I rewrite the article, I would make sure that the keywords "Crystal Cruises Luxury" are used heavily within the first 500 words on the page and then throughout the article.

A page optimized in this fashion is guaranteed to serve ads relevant to the keywords Crystal Cruises and Luxury. After you do a number of pages on your own, you will begin to get the hang of it and develop a sixth sense about keywords and which ones are going to pay off. If you optimize a web page and it still isn't serving relevant ads, go to the Google search box and search your keywords to see what ads are being served there. If there are ads being served for your keywords, then you need to revisit your keyword density to make sure that other keywords are not overpowering your primary keywords. Later in this book, I will share a free tool that will give you a complete report on how to identify keyword conflicts.

Chapter Nine

Travel Affiliate Programs

While Google AdSense is one affiliate program that you can use to generate revenues from your website, there are many others from which to choose. In fact, there are so many affiliate programs that it would be hard to even start to explore them all within the confines of this book. You can find a more complete list of affiliate programs by visiting www.HomeBasedTravelAffiliate.com and entering the backroom. Not only are the listings more complete, they are also kept current as well.

There is never a charge to join an affiliate program, but your site(s) will need to meet certain parameters to be accepted by the company offering the programs. You will also have to agree to the "Affiliate Agreement" terms and conditions and act within the prescribed behavioral guidelines. No affiliate program will allow you to use spam e-mail as a marketing tactic, and they will generally describe the way that you can offer affiliate links on your website(s).

When considering an affiliate program for inclusion on your website(s), you will want to select the ones that are most likely to generate a meaningful income. Success depends on marketing products and services that will appeal to your customers and you can genuinely recommend. As an example, if you have written an in-depth article about why travelers should purchase travel insurance, you can drive traffic by way of an affiliate link. Concluding your article with a specific suggestion of a company that has the best pricing, service and all around product with an affiliate link to their website to request a quote may reward you handsomely but only if the company is all that you claim. In this instance, your primary choice would be to go with the company that actually fills the promise.

Another application using insurance companies would be to write an in-depth article about travel insurance and then critique each company that you offer in a list of travel insurance companies. Virtually every insurance company has an affiliate program and you could sign up for all of them and then offer comprehensive information to consumers about travel insurance that includes a directory of links to viable companies. In this scenario, you might get smaller checks from each of the insurance companies. Affiliate programs are offered by both affiliate networks acting as intermediaries and directly from individual companies. Following are some affiliate program options that you might consider.

The Affiliate Networks

Affiliate networks exist to bring those offering affiliate programs together with publishers that use affiliate programs. (That's you!) The networks offer one stop shopping for affiliates and turnkey distribution for affiliate marketers. While there are dozens of affiliate networks, here are the major players.

Commission Junction (www.cj.com): Commission Junction offers hundreds of affiliate programs, many of which are major companies. As an example, Carnival Cruise Line brands are offered by Commission

Junction along with a number of other travel related affiliate programs. It is free to join Commission Junction, and they will issue you one check for all of your affiliate earnings from all of their programs.

Link Share (www.LinkShare.com) Established since 1996, Link Sahare is one of the leaders in affiliate networks. Link Share offers hundreds of quality affiliate marketing opportunities and is free to join.

PPC Publisher Networks

While Google AdSense is currently king of the Publisher Networks, there are several that are coming on fast. These networks all offer something unique and there may well be situations where their offerings may be more suitable for your application. Here are the more important ones:

Shareasale (www.shareasale.com): Established in 2000, Shareasale has over 2,000 merchants plugged into their network. Offering a wide array of products (many travel related), you may select those that best suit your niche. All payments are consolidated from the programs you participate in, and are paid with one check by Shareasale.com.

Yahoo Publisher Network (publisher.yahoo.com**):** Overture was one of the pioneers of contextual advertising. After Yahoo's acquisition of Overture, Yahoo made a firm statement that they want to compete with Google's AdSense head-to-head. While still in Beta, look for the Yahoo Publisher Network to dramatically change the contextual advertising landscape when it is made available to everyone. Yahoo Publisher Network is currently available only for those sites that have a substantial number of page views.

Chitika (www.Chitika.com**):** Chitika is unique. While its format is contextual, it offers a product called "eMiniMalls". These eMiniMalls offer a complete presentation of a particular product or service and delivered based on the keywords that reside upon a webpage. The presentation can include text, audio and video. Check these out, as they have a high click-through rate based on their presentation.

AdBrite (www.AdBrite.com**):** AdBrite brings advertisers and publishers together in a way that enables advertisers to select exactly where there ads appear and publishers to control exactly what ads appear on their site(s). As a publisher, you can set your own PPC rates and also approve every ad that appears on your site. As an advertiser you can select exactly on which sites your ads appear. It is a great way to build your CPM.

Kontera (www.Kontera.com**)** Kontera offers PPC Revenue Share exactly the same way as AdSense. However, the ads are tied to certain keywords (known as "wordlinks") that exist on the page and appear as linked words rather than advertisements. Kontera is an excellent choice to run PPC ads on blogs.

Kanoodle Bright Ads (www.Kanoodle.com**):** Kanoodle has been around a long time and offers a publisher's program that is very much like Google's AdSense. While their indexing doesn't seem to be as effective as AdSense, they are a well established company in the PPC advertising/publishing business.

Search Feed (www.SearchFeed.com**):** Search Feed is an excellent alternative to AdSense and operates just about the same way (including geotracking).

Companies Offering Travel Affiliate Programs

There is a wide array of travel affiliate programs from which to choose. While there are literally hundreds of travel affiliate opportunities, rather than detail them in their entirety in this text, here is a simple overview of just some of the programs that are available. While some of these companies work directly with their affiliate partners, others offer their product through a network, such as the ones mentioned above. You can obtain a more comprehensive list, along with detailed information on each program at:

www.HomeBasedTravelAffiliate.com.

Home Based Travel Affilate

Company	Product	Commission
A Traveler's Blessing	Travel amenities	10-20%
Accor Hotels	Hotels	3-6%
Adventurous Traveler	Travel resources/guides	15-18%
Agoda Travel Network	Hotel tour operator	55% of net commission
AirfarePlanet.com	Air	3-10%
AirGorilla.com	Air	$10 per ticket
AirportService.com	Transfers/Transportation	$.19-.26 per lead up to $2.08 for complete search
AirTreks.com	Trip planner	$60-$90 per booking
Alaska Air	Air	$2.00 per ticket
AlertsUSA	Travel alert service	15%
All Hawaii Tours	Tours and activities	6%
AllRez.com	Hotels	50% of net commission
Aloha Airlines	Air	2%
Aloha Top Ten	Tours and activities	5%
Auto Europe	Car rental	10%
Avis	Car rental	3%
Away.com	Travel tools and guides	$.25-$2.00 per registration
BabyBoomerTrips.com	Tour Operator	$.07 per PPC
BedandBreakfast.com	B&B lodging	5% of gross sale
BirthCertificatePassports.com	Document service	20% per sale
BookingWiz.com	Fare search	Pay per Search (varies)
British Airways	Air	2% air / 4% vacations

Budget Rent a Car	Car rental	3%
Calendars.com	Travel calendars	10% base
Carlson Hotels	Hotels	5%
Cathay Pacific	Air	$15 air booking / $20 All Asia Pass
Cheap Tickets	General booking site	$4 air / $5 hotel / $1 car
Cheap Caribbean	Caribbean vacations	5%
CityEverything.com	Website City Directory	10%
CondoSaver.com	Vacation rentals	50% of net commssion
Cruise Direct	Cruises	$25 per transaction
Delta	Air	$3 per ticket
DestinationCoupons.com	Merchant coupons (free)	$.01 per click
Direct FX	Foreign currency exchange	$1.50 per transaction
Dollar Rent a Car	Car rental	5%
Duty Free Depot	Duty free products	12%
eTravelFlorida.com	Guides and attractions	$.75 per lead + commission on sale
Economy Travel	Air	3% of gross sale
ECTACO.com	Translators and electronic dictionaries	15 – 20 %
Elliot Beach Rentals	Vacation rentals	$10 per booking
Enterprise	Car rental	1%
Euro Adventures	Tours (Spain & Portugal)	8.5%
Euro Railways	Rail transport	30% of net commission
Euro Relais	Vacation rentals	4-10%

EuropeanRail.com	Rail transport	4%
Excursion Online	Tours and activities	8%
Expedia.com	General booking site	$2 air / 3% hotel / 2% car / $20 cruise / 2% travel package
Faremax.com	Air consolidator	Set your own commission
FindVacationRentals.com	Vacation rentals	$25-$55
Fox Rent a Car	Car rental	5%
Free Travel Brochures	Trip planning	AUD$.50 per lead
Funjet	Tour operator	5%
Go Cielo	Hotels	5%
GoCardUSA.com	Tours and activities	$6 per sale
GotoBus	Bus travel	3%
Group Travel Planet	Booking engine (groups)	5%
Hawaii Active	Tours and activities	5-7%
Hawaii Activities	Tours and activities	5%
HotelClub.com	Hotels	50% of net commission
Hotel-Hunters.com	Hotels	3%
Hilton Hotels	Hotels	3%
Hotels.com	Hotels	5%
HotelsCombined.com	Hotels	70% of generated revenue
HotelsCentral.com	Hotels	5%
IAN.com	Booking engine	50% of generated revenue
Infohub	Travel guides	$1 for every brochure order
InsureMyTrip.com	Trip insurance	$10 per referral

Intercontinental Hotels	Hotels	3%
IntouchSmartCards.com	GSM Phones and cards	10%
Irv's Luggage Warehouse	Travel accessories	10-12%
JustAirfare.com	Air	$10 per ticket
Kayak.com	Fare search	TBD
KeySource Consumer Alliance	Travel support services	12%
Krazycool	Travel accessories and apparel	10%
Limos.com	Transfers/transportation	20% per lead search submission
Lowfares.com	Fare search	$35-$50 per search
Luggage Online	Travel accessories	10%
Magellan's Travel Supply	Travel supplies	10%
MainTour	Vacation packages	$5 per mini-vacation referral / $1 per Coastal Vacation Club referral
Mapquest Mapstore	Travel tools	8%
Maps.com	Travel tools	7%
Marriott International	Hotels	2.1-4.5%
Maui Active	Tours and activities	12%
MGM Mirage	Hotels	3%
National Geographic Store	Travel products	10%
Octopus Travel	Travel services	5%
Official Travel Documents	Documents service	20% of sale
OneTravel.com	General booking site	$5 air / 4-5% hotel / 3% car / 3% vacation / $30 cruise / $50 vac. rentals

Orbitz	General booking site	$5 air / $6-12 hotel / $2 car / $22 cruise / vac. pkg. $12-24
PasPic	Document service	10% of sale
Passport Visa Express	Document service	15%
PassportsandVisas.com	Document service	15%
Priceline.com	General booking site	2%
Priority Partner	Tour operator	7-10% hotels / 7% tours / 5-10% events / $3-9 tickets / $1 per dining res
PriorityPass.com	Airport VIP lounge	$14 per sale
Pro Travel Gear	Travel products	10%
Pure Water 2Go	Travel supply	25%
Rail Connection	Rail transport	4%
Rail Europe	Rail transport	5%
Rand McNally	Maps & related products	10%
RatestoGo.com	Hotels	4% + set a fixed booking fee
Rentalo.com	Vacation rentals	$1 per registered lead
Rentals365.com	Vacation rentals	50% of net commission
SafariNow.com	Hotels (S. Africa)	25% of net revenues
Sightseeing World	Tours and activities	6-10%
ShoreTrips	Tours and activities	Varies
Shuttle Direct	Airport transfers	8% shared / 3% private

SquareMouth.com	Trip insurance	20%
SportsTraveler.net	Tickets and events	7% tickets / 3% travel pkg
Starwood Hotels	Hotels	2%
StubHub	Event tickets	8%
Sun Splash Tours	Tour operator (college)	5%
Suvana	Transfers/transportation	10% of total fare
SwimOutlet.com	Swimwear & accessories	8%
T-Minus Vacation Countdown Clock	Computer travel accessory	10%
T2-Global	Discount Air	$4 per sale
Terravision	Transfers (coach)	5%
TicketCraze	Event tickets	10%
TicketLiquidator	Event tickets	10%
TicketsNow	Event tickets	7%
Thrifty Rental	Car rental	varies
Tourcaster	Tours (self-guided)	20%
Tours to Go	Tours and activities	5%
Travel Intelligence	Hotels	50% net revenue
Travel Trace International	Travel Accessories	50% ($15 first tier/$3 second)
Travel Guard	Trip insurance	varies
Travel Insured	Trip insurance	varies
Travel Tools	Travel accessories	12%
Travelershop.com	Travel accessories	15%
Travelocity	General booking site	$2-5 air / 3-5% hotel / 2% car / $20 cruise
Travelopolis	General booking site	2%
TravelRes.com	Hotels	40% of net commission

Travelscape.com	Hotel and air	5% hotel / 2.5% air+hotel package
TravelWorm	General booking site	$5 per sale
Trip Advisor	Trip planner	50%
Tripplus	Travel card	$10 per sale
TripSync	Travel tool	$5 per booking
Vacation Home Rentals	Vacation rentals	20%
Vacation Outlet	Land and sea vacations	3%
Vacation Rentals	Vacation rentals	$2 per lead
Venere.com	Hotels	2% +
Viator	Tours and activities	5%
Virgin Atlantic	Air	1-3%
Visa HQ	Document service	$5 per sale
WeHaveSeats.com	Event tickets	10%
Well Wishers Int'l	Travel gifts	15%
Wired Destinations	Hotels	6% of published rate
World Choice Travel	Booking engine	7-10% hotel / 5% pkg / 5%car / $5-10 air / $7.50 insurance / 40% attractions
Wynn Las Vegas	Hotels	5%
Wyndham Worldwide	Hotels	3%
Zaptel.com	Phone cards	5%
ZHotelZ	Hotels	5%
4Vacations.com	General booking site	$2.75 per sale

Chapter Ten

Marketing Your Website

Having all the content in the world loaded with affiliate links is just an effort in futility if no one comes to read the content and click on the links. This brings us to the topic of how to drive visitors to your website(s) to generate a flood of click-throughs and subsequent revenue stream. There are many strategies for driving traffic to travel oriented websites, and much depends on the value proposition that your site offers. If you are both selling travel and generating additional advertising and affiliate revenue streams to supplement the total income from the site, this is the best possible scenario.

Based on the conversion ratio of your visitors to primary value proposition sales, advertising and affiliate revenues may be an excellent way to dramatically increase visitors to your site and subsequently increase your conversions. Many sellers of travel argue that they do not want to have their visitors know about their competitors, and they do not want to send them away from their site. Here are some typical objections and concerns, rebuttal responses and subsequent realities to consider.

It Doesn't Make Any Sense to Send Visitors to My Website to Another Website. Don't I Want Them to Stay?

This is at the very heart of the issue and manifests itself into comments like, "I don't want my clients seeing advertisements on the web", or "I don't want my clients leaving my website" and so on. Look, whether you like it or not, clients know how to use Google and they surf the web looking for information. There is no way that you can prevent this from happening. In fact, I suspect that clients find a willingness to connect them with the best information on the web as a major positive and a reason to award business to the site that offers this connectivity.

It is this simple. A client visits your site, evaluates your value proposition and either decided to make a purchase, return later or leave. There is no such thing as a client that logs onto your website and stays forever. Why not make some money when he or she exits, while at the same time, giving your client options that might result in his or her completing their search?

The contextual ads or affiliate links that are presented on any given page of your website are from advertisers that are the highest bidders for the dominant keywords that appear on your specific page. Because they are the highest bidders, their content is likely to be very relevant to the information that the visitor is seeking. The fact that they are choosing to leave your site validates the concept that they have not found exactly what they are looking for on your site. While you didn't make a sale on your value proposition, you did create revenue from what would have otherwise been a visit that had zero impact on your bottom line.

Reality #1: Evolve an effective exit strategy for your visitors that will maximize your advertising and affiliate income. Focus on click-through rates, yield and overall CPM rates to maximize revenues.

Why Would I Allow My Competition to Run Ads on My Site?

You don't have to. Most Advertising networks offer competitive ad filter that allows you to block ads that send traffic to your competitor's website. If you enter "example.com" into your competitive ad filter it will block ads from appearing for "example.com", "www.example.com" and all subdirectories of the website.

Reality #2: Use competitive ad filters to block your competition and also the domain names that sponsor low paying ads.

I am Currently Running a Google AdWords Campaign (Paying around $5 per Click). Common Sense Tells Me Not to Pay to Get Them to My Site Just to Send Them Away.

Look, if the visitor found you through a Google ad, then they are highly responsive to contextual advertising and tend to make better users of AdSense. They are either going to find what they are looking for on your site or not. Why not subsidize your AdWords budget with AdSense revenue? You will be able to afford more clicks if you reinvest the AdSense revenue into your AdWords campaign to generate even more traffic. If you can maintain your current conversion ratio of clicks to sales, you should be able to dramatically increase your overall revenues.

Reality #3: Expand traffic to your website by reinvesting your Google AdSense revenues into a contextual keyword advertising campaign.

I Am Running Google AdSense, But Not Making Much Money.

Managing AdSense revenues is a relatively simple task. It is a function of the traffic a site(s) receives, keyword optimization on each page, ad design and layout and the quality of the content that resides in a web.

Reality #4: Google gives you all of the answers that you could ever want to increase your AdSense revenue on their site. Visit https://www.google.com/support/adsense for tons of information, and study Google's "Heat Map" that gives you the most desirable (effective) zones for ad placement. By studying this heat map, I made one simple change to my AdSense program that increased my click-through rate by over 1%. The same concepts that work for AdSense also work for all of the other contextual publisher networks. The more familiar you become with contextual advertising, the more successful you will become.

How Much Money Can I Make as a Home Based Travel Affiliate?

Travel websites are in a unique position to exploit opportunities such as Google's AdSense program and other affiliate opportunities. The skill set that is required to organize and present complex and detailed research is exactly what is necessary to succeed. Consumers wanting to purchase from suppliers directly on the Internet represent an unbelievable opportunity for those that are able to make the shift to a new paradigm created by the development of contextual advertising. Six figure incomes are commonplace in this new environment.

Reality #5: If you can invest the time and funds to learn the skills required to evolve web content, your existing skill set can create meaningful additional revenues that may dramatically enhance your overall profitability.

Marketing Your Web Site

Contextual Advertising: When we think of marketing, we always think of advertising first. Of course, you should consider running a contextual advertising campaign to drive traffic to your site. But, be cautious to pay less for the keywords that you are bidding on than your average earnings per click. Let's say that you average $3.00 per click and have a click through rate of 5%. This would tell you that you are earning $15.00 per 100 clicks or $.15 per click. You can feel comfortable that if you ran a campaign buying relevant keywords for $.05 to $.10 per click, you could potentially drive up your profits by buying traffic, simply because your average per-click income is above your average per-click cost. Of course, you would need to closely monitor the performance of the increased visitors to make sure that the CPM, CTR and subsequent income per click rates stayed stable. One of the most desirable aspects of focusing on travel is the high bid rates for keywords and high CTRs imbedded in the travel category.

If your website(s) also offer a value proposition that substantially increases the yield per conversion (click to sale) to a much higher level (say $25.00), you can easily justify spending considerably more on contextual advertising. This is assuming that your conversion ratio stays the same. Here is how to impact your click to sale conversion ratio.

Use Landing Pages: If you are selling a 4-islands Hawaii tour for $995.00, use the words "to make a reservation, Book NOW!" or some other action oriented term that tells the visitor that they are going to be delivered to a page requesting them to spend money. Never use the terms "for more information" or some other generic term that does not invoke a sense of action and urgency. Once someone has clicked on the ad, be sure to send him or her to a landing page that is specifically designed to convert the click to a sale. The page should have only the information that is needed to complete the sale, but allow the visitor to access ancillary information they might need to make a final decision. Serve the information in a pop-up window that when closed, leaves the landing page to complete.

Use Keyword URLs for Your Landing Pages: By isolating your landing page away from your main website, you remove the likelihood that the visitor will get sidetracked looking around other content on your site. By using specific keyword urls, you can dramatically increase the number of clicks that you get. In turn, the higher percentage of clicks that you generate reduces the overall cost per click. Google specifically rewards popular ads by granting them a lower cost per click than those that are not as prolific. In the example of the Hawaii tour, I might use the URL 14DayHawaiiVacation.com or 995HawaiiVacation.com. The domain name tells the potential clicker that the information that resides at the URL is focused and serious. Plus, the URL is memorable so that they may not click but simply enter it into the command bar thereby saving the cost of a click.

Turn a Click Into a Relationship: Nothing works better than personal contact. You might try collecting an e-mail address, or better yet a telephone number, before disclosing all of the details of your value proposition. So many times, a telephone call is the difference between a conversion and just a click.

Blogging, RSS Feeds and Podcasting: The largest initial benefit that blogs offer travel affiliates is simply a by-product of the functionality of blogging. The term "blog" is a hybrid of the words "web" and "log". A Web Log (blog) is simply a very easy to use website that was designed as an online diary or daily log. Blogs were initially designed so that people could carry on fully interactive conversations, post daily content in an easy to access filing system or introduce a diary fully equipped to stimulate comments and communication. There are a number of places to set-up your blog. Google owns and operates a completely free blog site at www.Blogger.com. You can start with one here, however I would suggest paying a nominal amount monthly for a commercial blog such as the one located at www.TypePad.com. The reason for this is you can assign a separate domain name to the blog and also enable an RSS (Really Simple Syndication) feed for the blog.

Search engines love blogs because they tend to be updated often and generally contain current and relevant information. Many people subscribe to RSS feeds to keep up on their blogs and websites, so it is a great way to keep your readers posted on anything new and exciting. The best way to use a blog is to post new activity daily and simply give a highlighted description with a link back to your web site for the complete details. While you can now include AdSense on your blog posts, it is much better to direct them to an optimized page on your website where they will be exposed to more advertisements and opportunities to click. Folks that subscribe to your "feed" will be notified every time that you update your blog.

Many people are using podcasting to garner traffic, but unless you have (or have access to) a professional speaking voice, podcasts are likely to cause more damage than positive results. While blogging was once a very quick way to get search engines to find you, at this point, there are now so many blogs that it is much more difficult, but still worth the effort.

eNewsletters: Enewsletters can be very effective in driving traffic. The key to using an enewsletter is to only offer an opt-in /opt-out format. Your readers should have complete control over his or her subscription. When it comes to enewsletters, it is content, content and more content that matters. Never waste a reader's time and energy by including old or redundant content. Your newsletter should be current, precise and meet the vital needs of your readers. The entire function of a newsletter is to drive traffic back to your website in droves. There are several companies that offer the service of maintaining opt-in newsletter lists and delivery. I use www.NetAtlantic.com and couldn't be happier with their service. They maintain a list that I can edit, add names to, search and to whom I can send both textual and html e-mail. Although I can send mail as often as I want, I have found that two newsletters a month is an excellent tempo. You can start your newsletter by rewriting your blog entries and invite folks that visit your site to join. Since your objective is to drive traffic and not sell anything, do not require anything more than an e-mail address to receive your newsletter. People tend to be uncomfortable about giving personal information when it is not necessary.

Write Articles: Earlier in this book we discussed the various sources of free content made available by authors that are allowing their articles to be used by virtually anyone. They do this because the agreement is that the author's signature is attached to the article. The signature is sure to contain an active link back to the author's website, and if the article is meaningful, will generate traffic everywhere it is published. You can take advantage of this wonderful opportunity to have your travel articles published all over the web by other travel affiliates looking for content to publish. It is a win-win situation for all parties. The more that you submit, the more opportunities you have for free traffic.

Links: Reciprocal linking is another win-win situation. The links will not only generate more traffic to your site, they will also improve your search engine ranking. Each page on the Internet has a page rank. Pages are ranked from 1 to 10. A page rank of 1 is inconsequential while a page rank of 10 is considered huge. The White House website home page is a page rank 10, and if it linked to your site, you would immediately be in the number one position for your keywords (or the keywords used to link to you). The best commercial websites are page rank 4, 5 and 6 (with very few 7s). Government and educational sites populate the higher page ranks. One link from a page rank 5 is much more important than a number of links from page rank 1 or 2 sites. Search engines view links from popular pages to be much more important than links from insignificant pages. One-way links (not reciprocal) links from high-ranking pages are the most important.

The key to obtaining high-value links is to focus your link activity on select sites that meet your criteria in terms of keyword relevance and page rank. Later, I will share a free tool that you can use to identify high page ranked sites that are compatible with your objectives. Once identified, invest whatever it takes to obtain the links. One excellent idea is to have a link site on a separate server from which you link to the sites that you are romancing for a link back. Instead of a simple link, build an entire page about the site's products or services and give them a first hand testimonial. Any website entrepreneur will appreciate this kind of link, and when you point out that it is a one-way link that search engines find extremely valuable, they will usually be responsive to your request for a return link to your home page using the specific keywords that you suggest.

If that doesn't do the trick, pick up the telephone and call the owner of the site and evolve a relationship. Explain that you want a one-way link from their site and inquire as to how you can make it happen. One never knows what deals are possible. Developing inbound links is a never-ending process and is well worth your investment of time and effort. Not only do the links build your site's popularity with search engines, but each link is capable of delivering a good number of people to your site based on the keywords in your link.

Online Communities: Many people overlook the obvious opportunity of driving traffic to their site by participating in online communities. Virtually all social networking sites have keyword searches of their members. As an example, let's say that your website deals with cruises and cruising. You can join MySpace.com, establish a formidable profile based on your cruise experience and ascertain several cruise oriented keywords that will be used to find you. At that point, when someone enters "cruise", "cruiser" or "cruise specialist" into the member search, you are included in the search results. When the person searching reads your profile, they actually get a well organized page built to have them visit your cruise site for tons of content for which they may be looking. It rarely costs anything to join social networks, but the results can be fantastic. There are numerous companies that will build an HTML page for MySpace.com for a nominal amount of money, and it is worth the investment to present a professional page to your visitors.

Bulletin Boards, Discussion Groups and Chat Rooms: These offer another wonderful opportunity to drive business to your site, but I must caution you that each community has a different tolerance for advertising (even the most subtle advertising). You should lurk in the group for a period of time before posting. Once you decide to post, begin with the most professional responses to questions that you can compose. After several posts and not before community members have become familiar with your presence and consider you a part of the community, should you include a link in your preferred signature file. Once the .sig file is included, it will propagate throughout all of the posts that you have made in the group. If anyone complains or says anything about it (even in jest), remove it at once and wait for a period of time. Still remain active in the group, and after a while e-mail the Administrator as regards the links you see in other signature files. Explain that you removed yours when someone made a negative comment, and ask what the group's formal policy is regarding .sig files. The Administrator is likely to tell you to include it, because he or she knows that if they refuse, you will move on and it is their job to grow the group. When they review your proliferation of posts and see their quality, you are usually given substantial latitude in whatever you choose to post. But again, never openly solicit or spam an online community, as this will immediately cause the Administrator to take action.

Reviews: Review sites can be an extremely valuable resource for driving traffic to your site. As an example, after a cruise, write a thorough review of the ship and the ports. You can write one large cruise review and then separate the review into segments covering each of the ports of call. Be sure to include many references to your website (potentially several different pages with relevant content), but do not insert active links. Review sites are wary of reviews that look too much like advertising and will generally not post reviews with active links and/or signature files with links or email addresses. The very best way to include your web address is to end your review with something like, "If you have any questions or wish further information about (topic), be sure to visit my DomainName.com site". This tells the reader where to go without inserting an active link. Once you have completed the reviews, submit them to every review site that you can unearth. It was not uncommon for a review of a popular ship at my CruiseReviews.com site to be read over 20,000 times in its first year on the site. This is a lot of exposure to a focused market and well worth the time it takes to write the review. By the way, you should also put your review (with pictures) on your website and include the fact that the complete review, including pictures, can be seen at YourDomain.com.

Viral Marketing: There are multitudes of different ways to get your site in front of people, and many of them can do more damage than good. Never propagate spam from your site in any form. If your site is reported spamming, virus software can warn a potential visitor that your site is a known spam site (or worse). Never harvest email addresses for the same reason. In order to take advantage of viral marketing, you need to devise a strategy for giving people something they want for free.

Here are some examples: If you visit www.CruiseTickers.com you can construct countdown clocks to be used with your discussion board .sig files for absolutely no cost. This is a simple .php application, but it has been altered so that it includes a link that can point to any site on the Internet. Another site that I am building, www.CruiseClocks.com uses a banner and a slider. When someone sets the clock, a cruise ship sails towards their departure date. This clock randomly rotates three different URLs that are tied to the clocks. There are currently thousands of CruiseTickers.com clocks in circulation at just about every cruise discussion board on the Internet, and I can change the site that they point to at will. Since these clocks are seen by everyone that reads the forums, they also see the message that directs them to whichever site I choose to put in place.

One of the most intriguing aspects of the web is its explosive nature. If you can come up with something people want and it is free, you stand the chance of driving an incredible amount of traffic to your site.

Refer a Friend: Always include the ability for someone to send an email to a friend with a link to the page they are reading or to sign up a friend for your eNewsletter, blog or RSS feed. Every time I send my newsletter, I immediately get a large bump in the flow of new members that subscribe. The opportunity to "Refer a Friend" is a motivating way for people to share quality information with others that they think would also be interested in the content.

Traditional Marketing: Obviously, you should include your website information on your stationery, business cards and traditional advertising. But, don't stop there. Think of other creative ways to generate interest. My son uses stickers to tout his www.SanDiegoSurfers.com site. As a community site, members can spread the word by putting really cool stickers on their cars, surfboards or wherever else they deem applicable. I see them everywhere in San Diego, and they drive traffic like there is no tomorrow. The only way that you can get them is by becoming a community member, and since they are considered "really cool", people join just to get the stickers.

When I owned www.CruiseReviews.com, I had baseball caps with the CruiseReviews.com logo embroidered upon them. These high quality caps were very well received and became a coveted possession. Since the cruise lines were aware of the site, people wearing the caps tended to be recognized and got excellent service while on board a cruise ship. The caps were not for sale, and the only way that one could be obtained was by entering and winning one of the weekly contests held by the site. I always wore one when cruising, and every time I got into a Jacuzzi with others, the conversation came around to the site. With each Jacuzzi encounter, a few more people became aware of the site and chose to visit it when they got home. Think of ways to expose your site in unique and positive ways, and the rewards can be significant.

Home
Based
Travel
Affilate

Chapter Eleven

SEO, Search Engine Optimization

Wouldn't it be great if every person that went on the Internet looking for a Caribbean Cruise in a search engine was delivered to your web site? Let's say that you could make this happen. Would you be willing to invest the time to accomplish this? Now, what if I told you this could happen with absolutely no investment? Sound intriguing? Impossible, you say! Well, read on and you will discover exactly how this can be accomplished.

We already know that potential visitors use search engines to find the specific information they seek, and they use keyword phrases to define their search. When the search engine displays the results of the search, remember, there are two types of links offered: The contextual advertisement links that have paid for the position at the top of the page and the free links that follow based on search engine results. Most searchers tend to opt for the free links first, because they have learned that these may contain the most relevance to their keywords. How did these sites get the top ranking positions? Try a Google search using the term "Cruise Reviews". Note, out of the

3,810,000 responses, CruiseReviews.com is in the number one spot. While many of these points have been covered in other places in the book, here is a concise list of each of the components that went into achieving that number one position:

Keyword URL: We have already discussed domain names and the power of a keyword domain name. If at all possible, obtain the specific keyword domain name for the product or service that you are attempting to position at the top of the search engines' results. Each search engine ranks the importance of domain names differently, but there is still great value in its acquisition.

Keyword Link: While we discussed the importance of a keyword link for AdSense to deliver relevant ads, search engines also look at the hyperlink to determine the contents of the page. Separating the keywords with a hyphen or underscore makes the identity of the keywords quite clear and eliminates the need for the search engine to sort through a bunch of letters to make that determination, even though it is something of which they are quite adept. In the two sets of URLs that follow, you can easily see the difference: www.Home_Based_Travel_Affiliate.com/How_to_Optimize_Web_Pages.html and www.BecomeaTravelAffiliate.com/HowtoOptimizeWebPages.html. You can readily see the advantages to separating the keywords. One of the biggest challenges when using .php or .asp technology is the automatic naming of the pages it creates. By the time the search engines work their way through dozens of characters, letters and numbers, it has a difficult time determining the subject of the page.

META Tags: META tags contain the information that search engines look for when they visit your site. Browsers do not display them, but here is how you can see what META tags your competitor is using to gain top search engine placement. First, identify your competition by entering your keywords in the search engine that you are interested in romancing. Once the results have been displayed, click on the link to the site in the number one free ranking position. Once the page has completely loaded, open your browser's "view" tool on the toolbar, scroll down to the "Source" or "Page Source" button and select it. You will soon be looking at the underlying HTML code that makes up the site (including the META tags). Notice that the page (all webs are the same) starts with a <html> tag, followed by a <head> tag. While browsers do not display this content, the <head> tag is what search engines seek out to begin to rank the page.

Following the <head> tag you will find other tags. Look for the <title>, <description> and <keyword> tags. This is the META information being offered to the search engines to obtain that #1 position. You can't copy this information for your own use, but you can use it for research. Look at all your competition to identify the common keywords, and start structuring your keywords around that keyword search string.

Your META tags should shout the specific keyword string to which your website is built to respond. Having a generic travel site that is not keyword specific will never allow you to get on top of the search engines. As you build and optimize your website, always think about the specific objective the site is trying to achieve and the keywords for which it is being built to respond.

H1 Headline: The H1 headline is the main heading of the page being crawled and is of the utmost importance to search engines. They see the headline as being major keywords for the page; therefore, it is imperative that your keywords appear here. I always use 18pt type just to make sure that the search engines understand that they are important. Never use a graphic for a page's headline, as using a textual headline is just too good an opportunity to reinforce your keywords.

Alt Tags: Using the .alt tags on all of your images can really help search engines zero in on your keywords. But, be very careful not to spam the keywords. Never use the same string more than 3 or 4 times on one page. Even then, be cautious. You are better off using them in different ways for each .alt tag.

Keyword Density: A major ingredient in achieving high search engine ranking is the density of the keywords that are used in the URL and META tags. By reaffirming that the site relates to the keywords, they should be the dominant keywords in the text portion of the home page. The major challenge is to write the keywords into the text for the search engines while still remaining an appealing read for your non-search engine visitors.

Link Popularity: One of the most important considerations by many search engines (especially Google) is the site's link popularity. Search engines love it when they crawl a site and find hundreds of links from other sites connecting to the site they are crawling. If there is a link from a page that is especially popular, this is considered particularly important and you will gain a higher ranking. The search engines do not make the distinction between sites that you own and those that you don't, so this is one very motivating reason to maintain several sites rather than just one.

Web Environment: In order to gain high search engine placement, your site should reside on a commercially viable host server. Free web sites or sites residing on servers known for their non-commercial content, will not be crawled, or if they are, will be deeply penalized. Further, you should strive for at least 20 pages of content to get the search engines attention.

While this is a brief overview of the elements necessary to gain high search engine ranking, rest assured that you could work your way up the hierarchy into the number one spot in any search engine. If this information interests you, here are some excellent sites to explore. In my opinion, the best site to investigate for information on search engine optimization is www.BruceClay.com. This site is the end-all on the subject, and it is well worth your time and effort to understand its content. The site offers numerous free tools you can use to examine your site and your competitors'. Another excellent site is www.SearchEngineWatch.com. This site will keep you in touch with the entire search engine optimization industry.

Gaining the number one spot in the search engines for your particular keyword search string has the potential to bring you unimaginable opportunities. If you see your web presence as a major part of your future, then search engine optimization will be a major consideration. For those of you interested in pursuing this opportunity, I have provided a brief overview of 10 things search engines love and10 things search engines hate.

10 Things Search Engines Love

There is no mystery to understanding SEO, but many sites are simply not friendly to search engines. So, without being too redundant, here are 10 things search engines love:

Use a Keyword URL: If your site is about bone fishing in Cozumel, Mexico, you should opt for the keyword URL Bonefishing-Cozumel-Mexico.com. You should also purchase the URL BonefishingCozumelMexico.com. Use the non-separated URL as your website address, but submit the separated URL to the search engines. They will see the keywords as separate words and will rank your site higher because of the keyword url.

Optimize Your Title META Tag: While META Tags are not the panacea they once were; you should carefully optimize your Title META tag to reflect your website's primary keywords.

Optimize Your Description META Tag: You should also optimize your Description tag to reflect your site's primary keywords and secondary keywords. It is important that the Description Tag reads in complete sentences rather than simple keywords. \

Optimize Your Keywords META Tag: Use WordTracker (www.WordTracker.com) to identify a list of keywords relevant to your site's primary keywords. Following your primary keywords, select keywords with a high KEI rating and structure them with the highest KEI ratings first. A KEI rating is a rating assigned to keywords by WordTracker that indicates the popularity of keywords when compared to how many times they are used on websites on the Internet. The higher the KEI rating, the more likely that you are in gaining a high ranking for the keyword in a search engine.

Use Alt Tags for Your IMG Files: Search engines cannot see .jpeg, .gif and .png images that reside on your website. HTML offers the opportunity to enter text in the Alt tag so that the search engines can identify the image. Using your primary keywords in your Alt tags is another way to tell search engines what your webpage is all about.

Use H1 Textual Headlines Rather Than Graphics: While using a textual Alt tag on a graphic is good, using a textual H1 headline is much better. The H1 headline is the primary headline on your webpage and is something at which search engines look closely. Use your primary keywords in your H1 headline to further help the search engines to determine the subject and contents of your site.

Use Textual Hyperlinks Rather Than Graphics or Java: Those fancy java-effect graphic buttons that change color and size when you roll over them with your mouse are really cool, but, unfortunately, search engines can't see them. Using keyword textual links is the way to proceed. Be sure to use the specific primary keywords for the page to which you are linking, as search engines give this a very high priority. Also, be sure to put a complete textual navigational structure on the bottom of each page in your website to gain maximum keyword penetration, and make sure that external links (from other websites) use your primary keywords.

Use a High Degree of Keywords in the First Paragraph and First 500 Words on Your Webpage: Make sure that your primary keywords are repeated consistently within the first Paragraph and the 500 words below your H1 title. Keyword density is critical in gaining high search engine rankings.

Optimize Each Page in Your Website for Unique Keywords: Google treats each page in your website with equal value. That means each page of your website stands a chance to gain top ranking based on its dominant keywords. By picking keywords with high KEI ratings, you should be able to move each page up in their rankings by optimizing pages for their own specific primary keywords. It makes no sense to optimize each page in your website for the same keywords, as each page offers another opportunity to gain visitors from the search engines that are using various keyword search strings to find information.

Update Your Web Frequently: Just like reading today's newspaper is more interesting than reading one two-weeks old, Search engines (Google, in particular) love it when they see that the web page is fresh and / or recently updated. The more often you update the web, the more likely that you will receive a higher relevancy ranking.

10 Things Search Engines Hate

The above information identified 10 things that search engines really like, so in this section we will explore things that search engines really don't like at all. Unfortunately, many web designers do not understand search engines and build sites that are pleasing to the eye rather than being search engine friendly. Gaining high search engine rankings can catapult you into rapid success. So, if you want to be successful on the web, understanding the nature of search engine optimizations is critical to your future. As you build and optimize your site, avoid these 10 deadly mistakes.

Forget Framed Websites: While framed sites can be really cool, the frameset that creates them is like speaking Greek to search engines. First of all, it takes thousands of characters to set up the framed site, and search engines looking for keywords can't find any. Then, the content that appears on the framed site actually resides on subsequent pages and is simply served to the frame set. While one can still optimize the pages served to the frame set, they simply do not carry the same weight. If search engine optimization is in your future, avoid framed websites.

Use Textual HTML Links, Not Java: Using Microsoft's themed navigation system or other Java written links will cost you dearly. Not only can't the search engines understand the intent of the Java graphic, they can't see the link itself. Search engines hate it when they cannot decipher the contents of a website.

Flash is Really Stunning, but it Will Cost You Big Time With the Search Engines: Once again, that Flash introduction to your website will cost you dearly. The search engine comes to you home page to find information about the keywords that identify the content on your site. Confusing them with a spectacular Flash introduction will only leave them unimpressed. If you must use a Flash intro to your site, consider having two URLs. One for your Flash intro and the other for your website. You can link them so that visitors can bypass your Flash intro and bookmark your HTML website if they choose to do so.

Use Textual Links, Rather Than Image Maps: Everyone likes those cool image maps where you can click on a section of the picture to visit the topic of the image and then roll over to another part of the picture to discover something different, but you will also be penalized big time for their use. Image maps are great design elements, but the search engines hate them. While the URL for the link can be determined, there are no keywords for the search engine to evaluate, thus leaving the search engine scratching its head.

Do Not Use Redirect, Doorway or Forwarded Pages: Search engines hate it when they crawl a page only to be redirected to another page automatically. Once considered a trick to fool search engines, this tactic is now the kiss of death. Do not put up one-page websites optimized for certain keywords and then try to redirect the search engine to another website that utilizes a different set of keywords. It won't work.

Do Not Try to Trick The Search Engines: All web entrepreneurs have heard of the tricks one can pull on the search engines to fool them into thinking the site is more relevant. Here are some of the most common tactics to avoid:

•Place your keywords in the smallest type and in the same color as the background of the website hundreds of times on a page so that the search engine will think the site is highly relevant to the keywords, but visitors cannot see them.

•Using unrelated keywords to the page's content. By using the hottest keywords for the day, one can quickly rise in search engine popularity. Yet visitors immediately see that they have been duped, and there is no benefit for the website other than a ton of page views.

•Duplicating websites will cost you big time. If Google finds a site with duplicate content, it will ban you from future searches.

Search Engines Hate Spam: Loading up your website with keywords simply to convince the search engines that your site is relevant to the keywords (spamming) will not work in the long run. The only way to gain keyword recognition is with density in your quality content.

Using Hidden Links: This technique involves placing hidden links (very tiny or invisible text links) on a home page knowing that search engine spiders will find them and index the source code. Once again, this is a technique that search engines hate. It's much better to build a site map to accomplish the same objective. A site map is a page on your website that is nothing more than a list of links to all of your separate Web pages.

Using "Submission" Services: A company that guarantees that your site will be submitted to 10,000 search engines sounds great, but search engines hate them with a passion. The fact is that you may be ignored rather than crawled.

Irrelevant Links: While sticking a link to your site on every website you can think of sounds great, if they reside on irrelevant sites, the search engines will lower your ranking. If you want to win over a search engine, you should only solicit links on relevant sites with high page ranks.

Summary

The bottom line is that there is no shortcut to gaining top search engine placement. Only through the constant and vigilant evolution of quality content, properly optimized for specific keywords will a site rise to the top. But, the rewards for arriving at the top are hundreds (even thousands) of free visitors that arrive at your doorstep at no cost to you. They are looking for quality content focused on the keywords they have put into the search engine, and search engines want to deliver it to them, as their popularity depends on it. If you offer quality content, they will find you. If you offer anything short of that, they probably will not.

Home Based Travel Affilate

Chapter Twelve

Bringing it All Together

We have explored the opportunity to become a home-based travel affiliate and delved in to the many aspects of achieving success in this exploding market.

... Global communications, global settlement and the web have created an opportunity for everyone to participate in global commerce on every level.

... Contextual advertising has made it possible for even the smallest marketer to reach local, regional, national or global markets with rifle-like accuracy and cost effectiveness.

... Global advertising networks feed contextual advertising to virtually everyone that uses the Internet. Keywords drive the network's accuracy and efficiency for the advertiser.

... Affiliate marketing has ushered in a pay-for-performance environment that serves advertisers and consumers alike. Publishers of content on the Internet can cash-in on the affiliate boom and create meaningful revenue streams.

12-2

Home Based Travel Affilate

... Technology has enabled anyone to build, publish and maintain professional and content rich web sites that are keyword oriented and optimized to serve contextual advertising and affiliate programs. Travel is the largest beneficiary of this tremendous opportunity.

... Folks with a deep interest in travel have access to tens of thousand of pages of free content and can also create their own. Not only does every travel supplier have volumes of information, resources and web content that they make freely available for travel professionals to use, but there are also numerous independent channels that offer content. This evolution of content is one the major opportunities that exists for the home-based travel affiliate.

... Community plays a huge roll in the future for contextual advertising and affiliates. Creating and operating an online community is a valid and actionable opportunity and worthy of exploration in a variety of formats.

... Google's AdSense offers new affiliates the opportunity to immediately monetize sites and create a revenue stream that can be built-on and managed. The task of optimizing pages for AdSense is easy to accomplish.

... In addition to contextual advertising publisher network opportunities, there are hundreds of other travel affiliate opportunities that can be incorporated into websites to drive major revenue streams.

... There are dozens of ways to market your websites to take advantage of free traffic to build site visitors. There are also several viable advertising and viral marketing opportunities to profitably create additional traffic that are valid considerations.

... Finally, SEO is a learned skill that is something any website publisher can master with just a little effort that will reap huge rewards.

The Opportunity

You can design, create and publish your own content-rich, travel-oriented website that will create a meaningful revenue stream. Simply, utilize your own content, as well as public domain content and optimize the pages to serve relevant contextual ads and you are well on your way to embarking on a successful business endeavor. The more content, the more profits. You can manage your contextual advertising programs for maximum click-through-rates and CPMs. You can increase your profitability by offering travel affiliate programs focused on the content you have published. You can effectively market your travel website(s) using viral, SEO and PPC marketing opportunities to drive traffic in ever increasing amounts to your website(s) in order to maximize profits.

If you are a travel agent, you already possess the skill set necessary to accomplish success in this new entrepreneurial opportunity and only need to learn the technological skills to design, create and publish websites. This should be a relatively manageable task that will reward you with an excellent income. You probably have drawers of content that can be converted to your website and have access to tons more.

If you are not a travel agent, I would strongly suggest that you take a look at my books on the subject, as you are probably already building websites and content, but may have limited understanding of the travel industry. Unfortunately, while most travel suppliers have volumes of content for travel agents to use to promote their products and services, they are not very sophisticated when it comes to supporting travel affiliates. You will discover how to take advantage of this burgeoning opportunity and maximize your revenue stream, by reading my book, "How to Start a Home Based Travel Agency". Through this book, you will gain an understanding of the travel industry and begin to realize the potential that exists for increasing your bottom line by being both a travel agent and a travel affiliate. Visit www.HomeBasedTravelAgent.com for more information.

While this book is a good foundation for establishing your presence in this market, the opportunity is still in its infancy and additional technology and venues continue to evolve. In order to access tons of additional information and resources about being a travel affiliate, be sure to visit the Travel Affiliate Resource Center. Very much like its relative the Travel Agent Resource Center, the Travel Affiliate Resource Center offers hundreds of travel affiliate opportunities, articles, links and information that all travel affiliates will find very valuable.

Glossary of Terms

Above the fold: Portion of the website visible when the page loads.

Affiliate: Partner or associate

Affiliate Networks: Entities that exist as intermediaries to bring those offering affiliate programs together with publishers that use affiliate programs.

ASP: Active Server Pages is Microsoft's server-side script engine for dynamically-generated web pages.

Backlink: A link from another website to your site.

Below the fold: The portion of a website that is visible only after scrolling.

Blog: A hybrid of the words "web" and "log". A Web Log (blog) is simply a very easy to use website that was designed as an on-line diary, or daily log.

Bulletin Boards: A discussion community that exists for the primary purpose of allowing members to discuss the topics of the various forums that exist within the bulletin board.

Click-through: The action taken when a visitor clicks on a web advertisement and is taken to the advertiser's website.

Contextual advertising: Advertising on a website that is targeted specifically to the person visiting the website.

Conversion rate: The average percentage of online visitors that take a desired action.

CPM: Cost Per Thousand ('M' is the Roman numeral abbreviation for thousand) is used by Internet marketers as a rate basis to price ads.

Crawl: The act a search engine performs as it creeps through a website.

CSS: Cascading Style Sheets is a code that is used to set standards for HTML websites.

CTR: Abbreviation for click-through rate

Dashboard: A website or servers control panel.

Deep link: Refers to a link on a website to a page on the site other than the home page.

Digests: A digest differs from a bulletin board in that members communicate with one another, but the posted messages are sent to every member in a digest format.

Dynamic packaging: Compiling dissimilar items from different suppliers and bundling the components into one transaction.

Feed: A shortened version of a web page document created for syndication.

Flash: Vector-based images or animations that are used on a website; animated graphic displays that appear when a site is loaded.

HTML: Hyper Text Markup Language is the code used to build basic websites. It defines the layout and structure of a web page.

Java: An object-oriented, high-level programming language.

Keywords: Words used by search engines in their search for relevant web pages.

Meta tag: The HTML command specifying how a document should be formatted that provides information about a web page.

Moderator: A community member that helps with one or more forums in an online community. Their function is to stimulate conversation and to enforce community standards.

PHP: Hypertext Preprocessor is a server-side, HTML embedded scripting language used to create web pages.

Podcasting: Similar to RSS in that it allows subscribers to subscribe to a set of feeds of syndicated web content. The difference is rather than reading the feeds, they are listened to via an iPod or similar device.

Portal: A website that offers a wide variety of services and resources.

PPC (Pay Per Click): An advertiser agrees to pay a publisher (affiliate) a fixed rate each and every time someone clicks on the link from the affiliate's website to the advertiser's site.

PPA (Pay Per Action): An advertiser agrees to pay an affiliate a fixed rate every time one of the affiliate's readers clicks on the advertiser's link and completes a stated action. This is also known as PPL (Pay Per Lead).

PPS (Pay Per Sale): This is a form of Revenue Share whereby no one makes any money until the consumer actually has an economic impact on the supplier. Once a financial transaction has been completed, the affiliate is rewarded by sharing in the generated revenue.

Referral Program: Another name for an affiliate program, a business arrangement in which a vendor pays someone a commission for referring customers to the vendor's site.

RSS: Acronym for Really Simple Syndication used to describe the standard for syndication of content for the web. It allows subscribers to subscribe to a set of feeds to view syndicated web content.

SEO: Search Engine Optimization is the process of increasing the number of visitors to a website by ranking high in the search results of search engines.

Spider: Also known as a "WebCrawler", a program that automatically obtains web pages and feeds them to search engines.

SQL: Structural Query Language (specialized language) for requesting information from a database.

URL: Uniform Resource Locator is the global address of resources and documents on the Internet.

Usenet: A global textual compilation of "Newsgroups" (same as bulletin boards) that are a venue for online communication and discussion.

User content: Refers to content that is created or submitted by those who use a site and is usually shared with the user "community".

Viral marketing: Refers to marketing techniques that use pre-existing social networks to produce increase in product awareness through self-replicating viral processes such as word of mouth.

VoIP: Voice over Internet Protocol enables people to use the Internet as the medium for transmitting phone calls.

VPS: Virtual Private Server space does not limit bandwidth and number of domain names that can be served.

Web 1.0: Refers to the period of time prior to the debacle of the dot com crash.

Web 2.0: Refers to the evolution of the next generation of technology that has occurred since the bust of the web in 2001.

Web optimization: Fine tuning your website so that it performs at its greatest potential.

Home Based Travel Affilate